The Economics of Public Issues

TENTH EDITION

Roger LeRoy Miller
University of Texas at Arlington

Daniel K. Benjamin
Clemson University
and PERC, Bozeman, Montana

Douglass C. North
Washington University, St. Louis

HarperCollins*CollegePublishers*

Acquisitions Editor: John Greenman
Project Coordination, Text and Cover Design: Heather A. Peres
Assistant Manager: Hilda Koparanian
Electronic Page Makeup: BookWorks
Printer and Binder: R.R. Donnelley and Sons Company, Inc.
Cover Printer: ColorImetry

THE ECONOMICS OF PUBLIC ISSUES, TENTH EDITION

Library of Congress Cataloging-in-Publication Data

Miller, Roger Leroy.
    The economics of public issues/Roger LeRoy Miller, Daniel K.
Benjamin, Douglass C. North.—10th ed.
        p.   cm.
    Includes bibliographical references and index
    ISBN 0-673-99460-0
    1. Economics. 2. Industry policy. 3. Economic policy
I. Benjamin, Daniel K., II. North, Douglass Cecil. III. Title.
    HB34.N6 1995
    330.973' 092—dc20   95-24753
                                                          CIP

95 96 97 98 9 8 7 6 5 4 3 2 1

To Jean-Baptiste and Marie,
Long summers in the City of Light are all that more
enjoyable because of you two.

R.L.M

D.K.B. dedicates this edition to Helen and Ernie Bolen,
with gratitude for their love, their kindness, and their
daughter.

Contents

Preface

This book is about some issues of our times. Several of these issues are usually thought of as being inherently noneconomic. Others provide classic illustrations of the core of economic science. Many are controversial and thus are likely to evoke noneconomic reactions to what we have say. In our view, however, the one feature that ties all of the issues together is that they illustrate the power of economics in explaining the world around us. And, we might add, we hope that all of them illustrate the fact that economics can be entertaining as well as informative.

Over the years, we have sought to select issues for this book that—in addition to the attributes noted above—possess a sense of immediacy. We hope you will find that the issues we have added for this edition meet this criterion. The new issues include the following:

- Rationing Health Care
- Inner City High Finance
- Getting Scalped
- The Economic Returns to Education
- Tired, Poor, Huddled Masses
- Disposable Workers
- Million Dollar Men
- The Effects of the Minimum Wage
- Smog Merchants
- The Value of Free Trade
- Floats, Fixes, and Crawling Pegs

All of the chapters in this edition have been partially or completely rewritten, and every chapter is, of course, as up-to-date as we can make it. What you will consistently find is a straightforward application of economic principles as they are taught in virtually all courses in economics, public policy, and the social sciences. This book can be understood by those who have taken a course in economics, are taking a course in economics, or have never taken a course in economics. In other words, we have made it self-contained, as well as accessible to a wide range of students.

You will find the chapters in this edition organized into seven parts. Part One examines the foundations of all economic analysis, including the concepts of scarcity, trade-offs, opportunity cost, marginal analysis, and the like. In a sense, the three chapters in this introductory part set the stage for the remaining twenty-seven chapters. The second through six parts of the book cover the topics—such as demand and supply, market structure, factor markets, and the impact of government policies—that are integral to virtually every course in which economics plays a role. At the end of the book, Part Seven examines the international scene, because international issues have become an essential part of the public issues of today.

Every part has a several-page introduction that prepares the reader for the material that is included in the following chapters. These part openers summarize and tie together the relevant issues, thus serving as launching pads for the analyses that follow.

Every instructor will want to order a copy of the *Instructor's Manual* that accompanies *The Economics of Public Issues*. In writing this manual we have tried to incorporate the very best of the teaching aids that we use when we teach from *The Economics of Public Issues*. For each chapter, the features of this manual are:

- A synopsis that cuts to the core of the economic issues involved in the chapter.
- A concise exposition of the "behind the scenes" economic analysis upon which the discussion in the text is based. For almost all of the chapters, this exposition is supplemented with one or more diagrams that we have found to be particularly useful as teaching tools.
- Answers to the Discussion Questions posed at the end of the chapter—answers that further develop the basic economic analysis of the chapter and almost always suggest new avenues of discussion.

The world of public issues doesn't stand still for very long. By the time you read this preface, we will be working on the next edition. If you have any particular subjects that you would like included in the future, let us know by writing us in care of HarperCollins.

Literally dozens of kind users of the last edition of this book, as well as several extremely diligent and thoughtful reviewers, offered suggestions for the current edition. To them all, we offer our sincere thanks and hope that the end result was worthy of their time and concern. We also thank Robbie Benjamin, whose editorial skills once again have improved the final product. All errors remain, of course, solely our own.

R.L.M.
D.K.B.
D.C.N.

Part One

The Foundations of Economic Analysis

INTRODUCTION

Our world is one of **scarcity;** we want more than we have. The reason is simple. Although we live in a world of limited **resources,** we have unlimited wants. This does not mean that we all live and breathe solely to drive the fastest cars or wear the latest clothes. It means that we all want the right to make decisions about how resources are used—even if what we want to do with those resources is to feed starving children in Third World nations.

Given the existence of scarcity, we must make choices; we cannot have more of everything, so to get more of some things, we must give up other things. Economists express this simple idea by saying that we face **trade-offs.** For example, a student who wants higher grades generally must devote more time to studying and less time to, say, going to the movies; the trade-off in this instance is between grades and entertainment.

Chapter 1, "Terrible Trade-off," examines a behind-the-scenes trade-off made every day on our behalf by the U.S. Food and Drug Administration (FDA). This federal government agency is charged with ensuring that the new prescription medicines that reach the market are both safe and effective. In carrying out its duties, the FDA requires pharmaceutical companies to subject proposed new drugs to extensive testing before the drugs may be introduced to the

1

market. When the FDA requires more exhaustive testing of a drug, this improves the chances that the drug will be both safe and effective. But additional testing slows the approval of new drugs, thus depriving some individuals of the ability to use the drugs to treat their illnesses. The drug approval process undoubtedly reduces pain and suffering for some people, and even saves the lives of others, because it reduces the chances that an unsafe or ineffective drug will reach the market. Yet because the process also reduces the rate at which drugs reach the market (and may even prevent some safe, effective drugs from ever being introduced), the pain and suffering of other individuals is increased. Indeed, some individuals die as a result. This, then, is the terrible trade-off we face in Chapter 1: Who shall live and who shall die?

If trade-offs, or choices are present in all of our activities, we must face the question of how we may make the best choices. Economists argue that doing so requires the use of what we call **marginal analysis:** the term *marginal* in this context means incremental, or additional. All choices involve costs and benefits—we give up something for anything that we get. As we engage in more of any activity (eating, studying, or sleeping, for example) the **marginal benefits** of that activity eventually decline: The *additional* benefits associated with an *additional* unit of the activity get lower. In contrast, the **marginal costs** of an activity eventually rise as we engage in more and more of it. The best choices are made when we equate the marginal benefits and marginal costs of activity; that is, we try to determine when engaging in any more of a given activity would produce additional costs in excess of the additional benefits.

In Chapter 2, "Flying the Friendly Skies?" we apply the principles of marginal analysis to the issue of airline safety. How safe is it to travel at 600 miles per hour 7 miles above the ground? How safe *should* it be? The answers to these and other questions can be explored using marginal analysis. One of the conclusions we reach is that *perfect* safety is simply not in the cards: Every time you step into an airplane (or even across the street) there is some risk that your journey will end unhappily. As disconcerting as this might sound at first, we think you will find after reading this chapter that once the costs and benefits are taken into account you would have it no other way.

Armed with the principles laid out in the first two chapters, we see in Chapter 3, "Choosing Crime," how they may be applied in yet another surprising venue: crime control. When politicians pat themselves on the back for how much they are spending on crime control, they are hoping you will ignore how much they are *not* spending; after all, as long as crime exists, there could be *less* crime. Of course, if we choose to have more crime control, we must have less of other things—trade-offs are present here, too. In the short run, having fewer burglaries may mean that we end up with more murders. In the long run, the trade-off may be that of accepting poorer schools in return for better law enforcement.

Chapter 3 also illustrates that the economic principles that are so powerful in understanding the operation of markets are also enlightening when applied to nonmarket settings, such as decision making by government agencies. Indeed, many governments are using the very economic principles we are discussing to make their agencies work more like private markets. We are led to conclude that in a world of scarcity, virtually every aspect of human behavior can be better understood through the application of the principles of economics.

1

Terrible Trade-off

How would you rather die? Due to a lethal reaction to a drug prescribed by your doctor? Or because your doctor failed to prescribe a drug that would have saved your life? If this choice sounds like one you would rather not make, consider this: Employees of the United States Food and Drug Administration (FDA) are making that decision on behalf of millions of Americans many times each year. More precisely, the FDA decides whether or not new medicines (prescription drugs) should be allowed to go on sale in the United States. If the FDA decides to allow a drug to be sold, doctors are free to prescribe it in the expectation that the beneficial effects of the drug will outweigh whatever adverse side effects the drug may have. But if the FDA prohibits the drug from being sold in the United States, doctors here may not legally prescribe it, even if thousands of lives are being saved by the drug each year in other countries.

The FDA's authority to make such decisions dates back to the passage of the Food and Drug Safety Act of 1906. That law required, among other things, that medicines be correctly labeled as to their contents, and that they not contain any substances poisonous or harmful to the health of consumers. As a result of this legislation, Dr. Hostatter's celebrated Stomach Bitters and Kickapoo Indian Sagwa, along with numerous rum-laden concoctions, cocaine-based potions, and supposed anticancer remedies, disappeared from druggists' shelves. The law was expanded in 1938 with the passage of the federal Food, Drug, and Cosmetic Act, which forced manufacturers to demonstrate the safety of new drugs before being allowed to offer them for sale. (This legislation was driven by the deaths of 107 individuals who had taken an elixir of sulfanilamide, which just happened to contain diethylene glycol, a poisonous substance usually contained in antifreeze.)

The next step in U.S. drug regulation came after the birth of numerous deformed infants whose mothers during pregnancy had taken a sleeping pill called thalidomide. When these deformities first became apparent, the drug already was widely used in Europe, and the FDA was moving toward approving it in the United States. In fact, about 2.5 million thalidomide tablets were already in the hands of U.S. physicians as samples. The FDA ordered all of the samples removed and prohibited the sale of thalidomide in the United States. Using this incident as ammunition, Senator Estes Kefauver secured passage of a bill known as the 1962 Kefauver–Harris Amendments to the 1938 Food, Drug, and Cosmetic Act. As it turned out, this legislation radically altered the drug approval process in the United States.

Prior to the 1962 amendments, the FDA usually approved a new drug application within a 180-day time limit, unless the new drug application failed to demonstrate that the drug was safe for use in the proposed manner. The 1962 amendments added a "proof of efficacy" requirement, and also removed the time constraint on the FDA. Thus, since 1962, manufacturers wishing to introduce a new drug to the market must demonstrate to the FDA's satisfaction that the drug is safe to use in the proposed manner, and also that the drug will accomplish the intended therapeutic outcome. Moreover, the FDA has free rein to determine how much and what type of evidence it will demand before approving a drug for sale, and it may take as long as it wants before either giving or refusing that approval.

The most noticeable impact of the 1962 amendments was a reduction in the number of new drugs coming onto the market. Indeed, researchers have estimated that the 1962 amendments cut new drug introductions by as much as two-thirds. This occurred because the amendments dramatically increased the costs of introducing a new drug and markedly slowed the approval process. Prior to the 1962 amendments, for example, the average time between filing and approval of a new drug application was 7 months; by 1967, it was 30 months; and by the late 1970s, it had risen to 8 to 10 *years*. Although the average approval time dropped somewhat during the 1980s, it still takes more than 10 times as long for a new drug to be approved as it did before the 1962 amendments. The protracted approval process involves costly testing by the drug companies and delays the receipt of any potential revenue from new drugs. Moreover, once all of the test data is in, the FDA may decide against the company's application. Overall, the expected profitability of new drugs has been reduced by the 1962 amendments, so fewer of them have been brought onto the market.

The rationale behind the FDA regulations is presumably protection of consumers, because generally consumers do not have the ability to obtain or analyze the information necessary to make accurate choices about the safety or efficacy of particular drugs. Consumers are at the mercy of the physicians who prescribe the drugs. But the physicians are also, in a sense, at the mercy of the drug companies, for it is almost impossible for each individual doctor to keep up with all of the technical literature about drugs and be aware of the advantages and disadvantages of each of them. Doctors must rely on the so-called detail people sent out by the drug companies to inform physicians about new drugs and give them samples to dispense to their patients, so that doctors can see for themselves how effective the new drugs really are. Because it costs drug companies thousands of dollars per physician each year to keep doctors informed about new drugs, the companies have an incentive to convince doctors to prescribe the drugs they make rather than the drugs made by competitors. Without FDA regulations, it is argued, the drug companies might introduce drugs that are not completely safe or simply do not work as well as they might.

Countering this argument is the fact that doctors, hospitals, and drug companies have strong incentives to prescribe, market, and produce drugs that are both safe and effective. After all, if it can be proven that side effects from a drug cause harm to an individual, or that an individual was harmed because a drug did not perform as promised, the ensuing lawsuit can cost the doctor, hospital, or manufacturer millions of dollars. Moreover, doctors, hospitals, and drug companies rely heavily on their reputations, and serious errors in prescribing, marketing, or producing drugs can damage those reputations beyond repair.

While debate remains over exactly how much FDA regulation is needed to ensure that drugs are both safe and efficacious, there is little doubt that the 1962 amendments have resulted in a U.S. "drug lag." The number of drugs marketed in the United Kingdom that are not available in the United States, for example, is very much larger than the number marketed in the United States that are not available in the United Kingdom. Although the FDA and its supporters note that it takes time to ensure that patients benefit from rather than are harmed by new drugs, regulation-induced drug lag can *itself* be life-threatening. Dr. George Hitchings, a winner of the Nobel Prize in Medicine, has estimated that the five-year lag in introducing Septra (an antibacterial agent) to the United States "killed 100,000, maybe a million people" in this country. Similarly, the introduction of a class of drugs called beta blockers (used to treat heart attack victims and people with high blood pressure) was delayed nearly a decade in this country relative to its introduction in Europe. According to several researchers, the lag in the FDA approval of these drugs cost the lives of at least 250,000 Americans.

Now we can begin to see the terrible trade-off in the market for prescription drugs: Although lives are saved because unsafe or ineffective drugs are kept off the market, the FDA regulatory process delays (or even prevents) the introduction of some safe and efficacious drugs, thereby costing lives. If the only cost of FDA-mandated testing were the millions of dollars that drug companies must spend on those procedures, there probably would not be many critics of the FDA, But the fact is that many persons could have benefited greatly—perhaps to the extent of being alive today—had the 1962 Kefauver–Harris Amendments not delayed the introduction of so many drugs.

With this thought in mind, let us take a more systematic look at the trade-off we face. Every time a new drug is introduced, there is a chance that it should not have been—either because it has adverse side effects that outweigh the therapeutic benefits (it is not safe), or because it really does nothing significant to help the individuals who take it (it is not effective). When such a drug is introduced, we shall say that a **Type I error** has been committed. Since 1962, incidence of Type I error—the thalidomide possibility —has been reduced by increasing the amount of testing necessary for the introduction of new drugs. People have surely benefited from this reduction in Type I error by incurring fewer adverse side effects and by being spared the costs of taking ineffective drugs. But other people have been the victims of what is called **Type II error.** Their cost is the pain, suffering, and death that occur because the 1962 amendments have prevented or delayed the introduction of safe, efficacious drugs. Type II error occurs when a drug *should* be introduced, but is not, because of FDA regulation.

Does the apparently high incidence of Type II errors by the FDA over the past 30 years imply that the regulatory process should be overhauled radically? Possibly, but even doing so would not eliminate the fundamental trade-off. The FDA's long, intensive review of new drug applications does produce benefits: the drugs that eventually reach the market are safer and more effective. As we have seen, the costs are that some safe, effective drugs never make it to the market, and many others are substantially delayed. Expediting the review process would enable more drugs to reach the market sooner, but it would also increase the chances that a harmful or ineffective drug might slip through the screening process.

It seems that for every benefit there is a cost. Indeed, this simple fact is so pervasive in our lives that economists have even coined a phrase summarizing it—*There is no such thing as a free lunch*—which simply means that in a world of **scarcity,** every choice we make entails a cost. By choosing to reduce the risk of introducing another thalidomide, we also choose to increase the risk of delaying another Septra or beta blocker. Trade-offs such as this are an inescapable fact.

The principles involved in making the best choices among trade-offs are discussed in Chapter 2. On the drug front, outcries over the growing incidence of Type II errors by the FDA have in some cases induced the agency to shorten the testing period for drugs when the costs of Type I error are insignificant compared to the possible damage due to Type II error—as is the case with terminally ill patients. Thus, over the past 15 years, the FDA has accelerated the approval process for several drugs used in treating patients with terminal diseases. One of the most famous of these drugs is azidothymidine (AZT), which emerged in 1986 as a possible treatment for AIDS. AZT received FDA approval after a testing period of only 18 months when it was found that the drug appeared to increase the life expectancy of AIDS patients. In effect, the FDA decided that the costs associated with Type I error—such as headaches, nausea, and a reduction in the number of disease-fighting white blood cells—were outweighed by the many deaths that would result if the drug were not approved quickly.

Despite this expedited review of AZT and a handful of other drugs used to treat AIDS or cancer, most of the agency's critics remain convinced that the FDA has too often and for too long weighed the terrible trade-off of drug regulation in a way that has produced tragedy for patients. As the battle against AIDS intensifies, there is little doubt that the pressure on the FDA to expedite the drug review process will increase. Only time and careful scrutiny will enable us to determine whether future choices by the FDA help us or harm us.

DISCUSSION QUESTIONS

1. Does the structure of the drug industry have any bearing on the types of errors that drug firms are likely to make? That is, would a drug industry comprised of numerous highly competitive firms be more or less likely to introduce unsafe drugs than would an industry comprised of a few large firms?

2. How could the incentives facing the people at the FDA be changed to reduce the incidence of Type II errors?

3. What would be the advantages and disadvantages of a regulatory system in which, rather than having the FDA permit or prohibit new drugs, the FDA merely published its opinions about the safety and efficacy of drugs, and then allowed physicians to make their own decisions about whether or not to prescribe them for their patients?

4. Suppose, for simplicity, that Type I and Type II errors resulted in deaths only. Keeping in mind that too little caution produces Type I errors, and too much caution produces Type II errors, what would be the best mix of Type I and Type II errors?

2

Flying the Friendly Skies?

Just about all of us hop into our car with little thought for our personal safety, beyond, perhaps, the act of putting on seat belts. Yet even though travel on scheduled, commercial airlines is 100 times safer than driving to work or to the grocery store, many people approach air travel with a sense of foreboding, if not downright fear.

If we were to think carefully about the wisdom of traveling 600 miles per hour in an aluminum tube 7 miles above the earth, several questions might come to mind: How safe is this? How safe should it be? Since the people who operate airlines are not in it for fun, does their interest in making a buck ignore our interest in making it home in one piece? Is government regulation the only way to ensure safety in the skies?

The science of economics begins with one simple principle: We live in a world of scarcity. As a result, to get more of any good, we must make some sacrifice of other goods. This is just as true of safety as it is of pizzas or haircuts or works of art. Safety confers benefits (we live longer and more enjoyably), but achieving it also entails costs (we must give up something to obtain that safety).

As the degree of safety rises, the total benefits of safety rise but the marginal (or incremental) benefits of additional safety decline. Consider a simple example: Having four exit doors on an airplane instead of three increases the number of people who can escape in the event of an emergency evacuation. Similarly, having five doors rather than four would enable still more people to evacuate safely. In both cases, more doors mean more people evacuated without injury, so the total benefits from safety rise with the number of doors. Nevertheless, the fifth door adds less in safety benefits than does the fourth door; if the fourth enables, say, an extra ten people to escape, the fifth may enable only an extra six to escape. (If this sounds implausible, imagine having a door for each person; the last door added will enable at most one more person to escape.) So we say that the marginal (or incremental) benefit of safety declines as the amount of safety increases.

Let's look now at the other side of the equation: As the amount of safety increases, both the total and the marginal (or incremental) costs of providing safety rise. Having a fuel gauge on the plane's instrument panel clearly enhances safety, because it reduces the chance that the plane will run out of fuel while in flight.[1] It is always possible that a fuel gauge will malfunction, so having a backup fuel gauge also adds to safety. Because having two gauges is more costly than having just one, the total costs of safety rise as safety increases. It is also clear, however, that while the cost of the second gauge is (at least) as great as the cost of the first, the second gauge has a smaller positive impact on safety. Thus, the cost per unit of additional (or incremental) safety is higher for the second fuel gauge than for the first.

How much safety should we have? For an economist, the answer to such a question is generally expressed in terms of marginal benefits and marginal costs. The economically *efficient* level of safety occurs when the marginal costs of increasing safety would just exceed the marginal benefits of that increased safety. Consider the example of doors on an airplane. Suppose that having a fourth door confers $1 million in benefits while the cost of adding the door amounts to only $300,000. The net benefit of having the door is $700,000, and, from an economic standpoint, it is efficient to have the fourth door. Contrast this with the prospect of having 13 doors on an airplane. Suppose that the thirteenth door confers benefits of $150,000 but that the cost of adding the thirteenth door is $900,000. In this case, the additional benefits of the door are less than the additional costs. Adding the door costs more than it is worth, so the door should not be added.

In general, the efficient level of safety will not be perfect safety, because perfection is simply too costly to achieve. For example, to

---

[1] Notice that we say "reduces" rather than "eliminates." In 1978 a United Airlines pilot preoccupied with a malfunctioning landing gear evidently failed to pay sufficient attention to his cockpit gauges. Eight people were killed when the plane was forced to crash land after running out of fuel.

be absolutely *certain* that no one is ever killed or injured in an airplane crash, we would have to prevent all travel in airplanes. This does not mean that it is efficient to have airplanes dropping out of the sky like autumn leaves. It does mean that it is efficient for there to be *some* risk associated with air travel. The unavoidable conclusion is that if we wish to enjoy the advantages of flying, we must be willing to accept some risk—a conclusion that each of us implicitly accepts every time we step aboard an airplane.

Changes in circumstances can alter the efficient level of safety. For example, if a technological change reduces the costs of manufacturing and installing airplane doors, the marginal costs of providing a safe means of exit will be lower. Hence, it will be efficient to have more doors installed, implying that air travel will become safer. Similarly, if the marginal benefits of safety rise for some reason—perhaps because the president of the United States is on board—it could be efficient to take more precautions, resulting in safer air travel. Given the factors that determine the benefits and costs of safety, the result of a change in circumstances will be some determinate level of safety that generally will imply some risk of death or injury.

Do airlines in fact provide the efficient level of safety? If information were free, the answer to this question would have to be "yes". Consumers would simply observe the levels of safety provided by different airlines, the prices they charge, and select the degrees of safety that best suited their preferences and budgets—just as with other goods. But, of course, information is not free; it is a **scarce good,** costly to obtain. As a result, it is possible that passengers are unaware of the safety records of various airlines, just as they may be unaware of the competency of pilots and the maintenance procedures of an airline's mechanics. The fact that information about safety is not free has been used to argue that it is appropriate for the federal government to mandate certain minimum levels of safety, as it does today through the operation of the Federal Aviation Administration (FAA).

The argument in favor of government safety standards rests on the presumption that, left to their own devices, airlines would provide less safety than passengers actually want to have. This might happen, for example, if customers could not tell (at a reasonable cost) whether or not the equipment, training, procedures, and so on employed by an airline are safe. For example, how many airline passengers are experts in metal fatigue, or are knowledgeable about the amount of training required to pilot a 747? If passengers cannot cheaply gauge the level of safety, they will not be willing or able to reward airlines for being safe or punish them for being unsafe. Consider a simple analogy: How much would you pay for a new set of clothes if the clothes were invisible? Not much, we would guess, unless you were an egotistical emperor. Hence, the reasoning goes, safety is costly to provide and consumers are unwilling to pay for it because they cannot accurately measure it; thus airlines provide too little of it. The conclusion, at least as reached by some, is that we should have a body of government experts—such as the FAA—set safety standards for the industry.

This conclusion seems plausible, but it ignores two simple points. First, how is the government to know what the efficient level of safety is? Assume for the moment that the FAA employs persons who are experts in metal fatigue, pilot training, maintenance procedures, and so on. Assume also that the FAA knows (1) the impact of these matters on the likelihood of deaths and injuries due to plane crashes, and (2) exactly how much it costs to implement various safety improvements.[2] The FAA still does not have enough information to set efficient safety standards because it does not know the value that people place on safety. Without such information, the FAA has no way of assessing the benefits of additional safety, and thus no means of knowing whether those benefits are greater or less than the costs.[3]

The second point is perhaps more fundamental. It is likely that people are really interested in reaching their destinations safely, and not in whether they got there because of a good plane, a good pilot, or a good mechanic. Even if they cannot observe if an airline hires good pilots or bad pilots, they can observe whether that airline's planes land safely or crash—if for no other reason than because air-

---

[2] Many people would argue that these assumptions presume that the FAA knows more than it could possibly know; we make the assumptions only to present the case for government safety regulations in the best light.

[3] Even if FAA experts know how much they benefit from additional safety, how are they to know how much you benefit?

plane crashes are the subject of intense media scrutiny. If it is *safety* that is important to consumers—and not the obscure, costly-to-measure set of reasons for that safety—the fact that consumers cannot easily measure metal fatigue in jet engines may be totally irrelevant to the process of achieving the efficient level of safety. If you know that an airline's planes have a nasty habit of hitting mountains, do you really care whether it is because their pilots have bad eyesight or because their planes have no altimeters?

Interestingly, evidence shows that consumers *are* cognizant of the safety performance of airlines, and that they "punish" airlines that perform in an unsafe manner. Researchers have found that when an airline is "at fault" in a fatal plane crash, consumers appear to downgrade their safety rating of the airline (i.e., revise upward their estimates of the likelihood of future fatal crashes).[4] As a result, the offending airline suffers substantial, adverse financial consequences, over and above the costs of losing the plane and being sued on behalf of the victims. Although these research findings do not guarantee that airlines provide the efficient level of safety, they do reveal that the market punishes unsafe performance—suggesting a striking degree of safety awareness on the part of supposedly ignorant consumers. If consumers (who are, after all, the ultimate judges of the value of their own safety) can accurately and cheaply judge the *outcomes* of the safety procedures followed by airlines, ignorance about the *nature* of those procedures may be irrelevant to the provision of the efficient level of safety.

We began this chapter by observing that, all things considered, air travel is considerably safer than automobile travel, a fact that has had a peculiar consequence in recent years. Air travel has become much less expensive over the past 20 years. As a result, consumers have been driving less and flying more; in fact, more than twice as many people are flying now as in to the late 1970s. Because traveling on scheduled, commercial airlines is roughly 100 times safer than driving an automobile, this switch in travel modes is estimated to have significantly reduced annual highway accidents, injuries, and deaths. Sometimes, fact really is stranger than fiction.

---

[4] Mark L. Mitchell and Michael T. Maloney, "Crisis in the Cockpit? The Role of Market Forces in Promoting Air Travel Safety," *Journal of Law & Economics*, October 1989, pp. 139-184.

DISCUSSION QUESTIONS

1. Is it possible to be too safe? Explain what you mean by "too safe."

2. Many automobile manufacturers routinely advertise the safety of their cars, yet airlines generally do not even mention safety in their advertising. Can you suggest an explanation for this difference?

3. Many economists would argue that private companies are likely to be more efficient than the government in operating airlines. Yet many economists would also argue that there is a valid reason for government to regulate the safety of those same airlines. Can you explain why (or why not) the government might be good at ensuring safety, even though it might not be good at operating the airlines?

4. Professional football teams sometimes charter airplanes to take them to their "away" games. Would you feel safer riding on a United Airlines plane that had been chartered by the Washington Redskins rather than on a regularly scheduled United Airlines flight?

3

Choosing Crime

How much is crime prevention worth? Plenty, apparently—at least in New York City, which spends over $1.6 *billion* a year on its police department. That works out to about $200 a year for each of the city's residents, or $800 for a family of 4. Why do New Yorkers spend so much on crime prevention? If the answer seems obvious, then why don't they spend even *more*? (After all, roughly 2000 murders are committed in New York City each year, and many residents there consider muggings and burglaries as much a part of life as rude taxi drivers.) Would spending more on the police department reduce crime in New York City? If it would, then why did the city council decide to permit so much crime—by spending only $1.6 billion? If such spending does not deter crime, why isn't the police department simply abolished, with the savings used to improve the city's decaying school system?

Before we can begin to answer these questions, we must look at the economics of fighting crime. First of all, it is not just the police that are involved in crime prevention. The courts and the prison system also enter the picture, as do devices such as burglar alarms, locks, and safes. Second, we start with the presumption that spending more on crime prevention makes it more difficult (costly) for people to commit crimes and for them to avoid detection and punishment. Thus, devoting more resources to law enforcement will, to some degree, deter crime.

Law enforcement has many aspects, and the costs of each must be considered in allocating the resources available. The costs can be divided into three general areas. First, there are the costs of crime detection and the arrest of suspects. Second, costs are incurred in the trial and conviction of the prisoner; they vary with the efficiency and speed with which the law enforcement officials and the courts can act. Third, once a sentence is imposed, there are the economic costs of maintaining and staffing prisons. (This third area and the so-cial implications of what types and durations of punishment are most effective as deterrents to crime are examined in Chapter 21.)

Even though an increase in the resources devoted to discover-ing and apprehending criminals can be expected to reduce crime, the optimum allocation of those resources is not so clear-cut. The chief of police or commissioner is faced with two sets of problems. He or she must decide how to divide the funds between capital and labor; that is, whether to choose more cars, equipment, and labora-tories or more patrol officers, detectives, and technicians. The chief must also allocate funds among the various police details within the department; that is, decide whether to clamp down harder on homi-cide, car theft, or drug traffic.

Within a law enforcement budget of a given size, the police chief must therefore determine the optimum combination of pro-duction factors. The ideal combination is one in which an additional dollar spent on any input will provide an equal additional amount of crime prevention. If an additional dollar spent on laboratory equipment would yield a higher crime-deterrent result than if the dollar were spent on a police officer's salary, the laboratory would win. While it is clear that the productivity of inputs is difficult to measure in such small amounts, this does not alter the basic argu-ment. Nor does it alter the argument to say that some inputs are *in-divisible*, that they come only in fixed, discrete physical units.[1] Usually the police chief must judge from experience and intuition as well as from available data whether buying more cars or hiring more people will do the better job in decreasing crime. This decision may change with changes in relative prices. For example, if the salaries of police officers increase, the balance may tip toward the use of more cars or equipment, depending on how well capital can be substituted for labor in a given situation. Instead of using two po-lice officers in a car, it might be efficient to equip the car with bullet-proof glass and let the driver patrol alone.

The police chief or commissioner must also determine how to allocate resources among the interdepartmental details. Sometimes highly publicized events influence this decision. For example, sev-

---

[1] A good or service is said to be indivisible if it can be sold only in relatively large quanti-ties. For example, one cannot purchase one-tenth of a police car. However, perhaps the car can be rented for one-tenth of each month. Given the possibility of rental, many prod-ucts can no longer be called indivisible.

eral years ago prostitution increased in downtown Seattle to such a degree that local merchants complained that streetwalkers were hurting business. The merchants induced the police chief to increase sharply the detection and apprehension of prostitutes. That meant using more personnel and equipment on the vice squad; within a fixed budget, this could be done only by pulling resources away from homicide, robbery, and other details. In effect, the cost of reducing prostitution was an increase in assault and robbery.

The second area of law enforcement that incurs costs is the trial and its outcome. Recent studies indicate that the likelihood of conviction is a highly important factor (if not the major one) in the prevention of crime. Currently, the probability of conviction and punishment for crime is extremely low in the United States. Nationwide, the odds of imprisonment for committing a crime are about 1 in 25. In New York City, it has been estimated that an individual who commits a felony faces less than a 1 in 200 chance of going to jail. Poor crime detection partly explains such incredible figures; court congestion adds to the problem. In big cities, the court calendar is so clogged that the delay in getting a case to trial may stretch from months into years.[2]

One consequence of this is an increasing tendency for the prosecutor and suspect to arrange a pretrial settlement rather than further overburden the courts. This is what happens with 90 percent of all criminal charges. Many observers believe that society is underinvesting in the resources needed to improve this process. If more were spent on streamlining court proceedings instead of on making arrests, cases could be brought to trial more promptly, the presence of all witnesses could be more easily secured, and the district attorney would not be forced to make "deals" with suspects. Faced with the probability of quick and efficient trial, a potential criminal might think harder about robbing a bank or mugging a pedestrian.

We can now return to our original question. How did New York City determine that a budget of $1.6 billion for crime prevention was the right amount? In the short run, the city was faced with a total budget of a given size and had to decide how to carve it up between law enforcement and other municipal demands, such as fire protection, health, parks, streets, and libraries. Just as a police chief

---

[2] Many court calendars are solidly booked for two, three, or even five years into the future. In New York City, for example, the average time lapse between filing a civil suit and getting it to trial is nearly three and a half *years*.

or commissioner must try to determine what combination of police officers and equipment within a fixed budget will deter the greatest amount of crime, a city council will attempt to choose a combination of spending on all agencies that will yield an amount of public services with the greatest value. If additional money spent on fire protection does not yield as much "good" as it would if spent on police protection, then the amount should be allocated to law enforcement. Determining the value of services rendered by each agency is difficult but not impossible, at least in principle. Crude approximations can be made of the benefits and costs of each activity, and the efficiency of the public sector can be improved as such calculations are made and refined.

The short-run constraint of a fixed budget for law enforcement may be altered in the long run by asking the state legislature for increased funds for crime prevention. The legislature will then have to wrestle with the same allocation problem that engaged the city council: Will spending an additional dollar on higher education yield greater returns for society than the same dollar directed to crime prevention? The same difficult questions arise in measuring the value of unpriced services resulting from any given state expenditure.

In general, the state will have greater latitude than the city council in raising taxes. If the state chooses to raise taxes, this will broaden the allocation problem. The increased taxes will reduce the disposable income of some part of the citizenry. Those who pay the additional taxes must decide whether the additional public services are worthwhile. For example, is the reduction in crime attributable to an increased expenditure on law enforcement as valuable to them as the goods they could have enjoyed from that increased tax money? If they do not think so, at the next election they may vote to "throw the bums out."

Our description indicates that nonmarket solutions to economic problems parallel market solutions. Although we have focused on crime prevention, the criteria are similar for all types of government decisions and for all levels of government—local, state, and federal. Nevertheless, certain differences must be noted between decision making in the private, market sector of the economy and in the public, nonmarket sector. Problems of measurement are much greater in the latter. How, for example, do we put a price tag on recreation, which is the output of the parks department? The signals come through much louder and more clearly in market situations, in which changes in private profitability directly indicate which policies will be best.[3] Instead of market signals, makers of public policy receive a confused set of noises generated by opponents and proponents of their decisions. A legislator is in the unenviable position of trying to please as many constituents as possible while operating with very incomplete information.

Some cities have tried to use market mechanisms to improve crime prevention. A few years ago, the city of Orange, California, near Los Angeles, started paying its police according to how much crime was reduced. The incentive scheme applied to four categories of crime—burglary, robbery, rape, and auto theft. Under the plan, as first put into effect, if the crime rate in those categories was cut by a certain amount during the previous year, the police would get an extra 1 percent raise. If the crime rate was cut even more, the pay increase would be an extra 2 percent. The results were encouraging. Detectives on their own time produced videotape briefings with leads for patrol officers on specific beats. The whole force developed a campaign to encourage safety precautions in residents' homes. Statistically speaking, the results were even more impressive, for during the initial phase of the program crime in the four target categories fell by almost *triple* the most optimistic goal. The other crime figures held steady, indicating that the police force was not merely shifting its efforts from one area of crime to another.

Let us consider a closely related matter. Until the early 1980s, in many cities and states a person beaten up in the streets and left with permanent brain damage could not sue for injuries. The attacker, if caught, would be jailed—but that did not help the victim, who ended up paying taxes for the prisoner's room and board! The first move toward compensation of victims of crime for their suffering was an initiative passed in California in 1982. This initiative was widely referred to as a "bill of rights" for crime victims. It required convicts to make restitution to those harmed (and also made other broad changes, such as putting limits on bail releases and insanity pleas). Since then, most states have established funds to compensate crime victims. Along the way, Congress passed the Victims of Crime Act, which enabled distribution of millions of dollars collected from

---

[3] In instances where **externalities** exist, it may be to society's advantage to alter these signals by appropriate measures.

federal criminal penalties and fines to victims' groups across the country.

For the most part, however, such compensation is far less than the full cost of the crime. What if a city or a state were responsible for restitution of the full cost of a crime committed within its borders? One might guess that unlimited liability on the part of government for crimes against the populace would certainly alter the present allocation of resources between crime prevention and other public endeavors.

This raises the question of what is called "moral hazard." If victims of robberies, for example, were fully compensated by the municipality, there would be less incentive for individuals to protect themselves privately against robberies. The same is true for other crimes. One way to avoid this "moral hazard" would be to establish a deductible on the municipality's liability. For example, for home robberies, the municipality might be held responsible for all losses in excess of $500. If this were the case, homeowners still would have an incentive to lock their doors, have watchdogs, and keep lights on at night when they are away.

Another way in which the allocation of crime prevention resources might be altered is demonstrated by a pilot project in crime prevention in Newport News, Virginia, a Navy port city with a population of about 160,000. Aided by a $1.2 million grant from the federal government, the police sought to deter crime before the fact rather than punishing it after the fact. At the heart of the program was a "crime analysis model," a lengthy questionnaire filled out by police officers whenever a crime was committed. Analysis of these reports over time enabled the police to predict, with a surprising degree of accuracy, where crimes were likely to be committed. Steps could then be taken to prevent the crime by drawing on other public and private resources, such as community health clinics, social workers, attorneys, and welfare agencies. By analyzing homicide cases over an 18-month period, for example, the police found that 50 percent of all the murders committed had involved family members of the victims and that in half of those cases the police had already received complaints of domestic violence. As a result, a new procedure was implemented. Police began making arrests whenever they witnessed domestic violence, without waiting for a family member to swear out a warrant. The arrested party was placed in jail and released only if the individual agreed to professional counseling. The counseling seemed to work: For the 5 years preceding the experiment, the city had averaged 25 murders per year—half of them the result of domestic violence. During the pilot program, the murder rate was cut by two–thirds, and domestic murders were reduced even more. In all areas of crime—prostitution, robberies, burglaries, and "nuisance" crimes such as petty theft and vandalism—similar prevention techniques have been used successfully.

Traditionally, police have responded to crime, rather than taking an active preventive role. The Newport News program involves a radical reorientation of the work of the police. The results of the experiment suggest that perhaps, if more money and resources were allocated to crime prevention before the fact, the high cost of crime might be reduced for victims and taxpayers alike. Crime costs. So does crime prevention. But the latter has benefits to society that should be weighed when making decisions about law enforcement methods and expenditures.

DISCUSSION QUESTIONS

1. Discuss the allocation of resources for nonmarket activities such as higher education, firefighting, and highway construction.
2. How does a private firm decide how to allocate resources? How does the decision–making process differ from that of a government agency?
3. Large cities generally spend more per capita on crime prevention than do small towns. Economists would suggest that this difference is due to differences in both the costs and benefits of (1) committing crimes and (2) preventing crimes in large cities compared to small towns. Can you suggest what some of these differences in costs and benefits might be?
4. Economists speak of economic agents (such as the chief of police in this chapter) making decisions as though they wish to maximize the net benefits of their decisions. Do individuals have to think in the same terms that economists do for our **theories** (or *models*) to be useful in explaining their behavior? (*Hint:* Fable has it that Sir Isaac Newton was stimulated to develop his theories about the laws of motion as a result of being hit on the head by an apple that had fallen out of the tree under which he was sitting. Did the apple have to understand Newton's theory to behave according to it?)

Part Two

Supply and Demand

INTRODUCTION

The tools of demand and supply are the most basic and useful elements of the economist's kit. Indeed, many economists would argue that the **law of demand**—the lower the price of a good, the greater the quantity of that good demanded by purchasers—is the single most powerful proposition in all of economics. Simply stated, the law of demand has the capacity, unmatched by any other proposition in economics, to explain an incredibly diverse range of human behaviors. For example, the law of demand explains why buildings are taller in downtown areas than in outlying suburbs, and also why people are willing to sit in the upper deck of football stadiums even though lower deck seats are clearly superior. The great explanatory power of the law of demand is almost matched by that of the **law of supply,** which states that the higher the price of a good, the greater will be the quantity of that good supplied by producers. The law of supply helps us understand why people receive a premium wage when they work overtime, as well as why parking places at the beach are so much more expensive during the summer months than they are during the winter.

When the laws of demand and supply are combined, they illuminate the enormous **gains from trade** that arise from voluntary exchange. In Chapter 4, "Sex, Booze, and Drugs," we examine what happens when the government attempts to prohibit the exchanges that give rise to these gains. The consequences are often surprising, always costly, and—sadly—sometimes tragic. We find, for example, that when the federal government made alcoholic beverages illegal during the era known as Prohibition, Americans responded by switching from beer to hard liquor, and by getting drunk a larger proportion of the times when they drank. We also show that the government's ongoing efforts to prevent individuals from using drugs such as marijuana and cocaine cause the "drive-by" shootings common in so many major cities, and also encourage drug overdoses among users. Finally, we explain why laws against prostitution help to foster the spread of acquired immune deficiency syndrome (AIDS).

In Chapter 5, "Is Water Different?" we dispel the myth that the consumption of some goods does not conform to the law of demand. Here, we examine the demand for water, that "most necessary of all necessities," and find that—lo and behold—when the price of water is raised, people consume less of it—exactly as predicted by the law of demand. One important conclusion of this chapter is that the "water shortages" and "water crises" that afflict various parts of the nation are not the result of droughts, but in fact are caused by government officials who are unwilling or unable to accept the reality of the law of demand.

Although the debate over health care seems far removed from the demand for water, Chapter 6, "Rationing Health Care," shows that key elements can be illuminated with economic principles. In response to the high cost of medical care, many nations have tried to remove health care from the marketplace. Yet the fundamental problems of scarcity remain: producers must be rewarded for their efforts, and consumers' otherwise unlimited desires must somehow be rationed. In the market system, prices perform these functions. But under the systems of government-mandated, universal health care that now exist (or are likely to exist), suppliers are directed by government edict and prices no longer ration demand. Instead, these systems rely on another method of rationing: It is called "rationing by waiting," because people are forced to wait—for weeks or even months—for whatever level of medical care that is offered them. Under such a system, the costs of health care are clearly different than they are under a market system, but it is not clear that they are any lower.

Medical matters also form the focus of our analysis in Chapter 7, "Choice and Life," where we look at an issue seemingly unrelated to economics—abortion. While the debate between a woman's right to choose and a fetus's right to live is usually cast in highly charged, emotional terms, we demonstrate that the dispassionate reasoning of the economist can illuminate some of the issues at stake. Although economics can never be the ultimate arbiter of whether abortion should be legal or illegal, it can help us understand more about what our choices cost.

Our final application of demand and supply analysis comes in Chapter 8, "Bankrupt Landlords, from Sea to Shining Sea." This chapter brings us back to the issue discussed in Chapter 4, the effects of government interference with free markets, in this case in the form of **rent controls**—legal ceilings on the rent that landlords may charge for apartments. Although the effects of rent controls are perhaps less tragic than some of the effects observed in Chapter 4, they are just as surprising, and often as costly. We find, for example, that legal ceilings on rents have increased the extent of homelessness in the United States, have led to a rise in racial discrimination, and have caused the wholesale destruction of hundreds of thousands of dwelling units in our nation's major cities. We cannot escape one simple fact: Politicians may pass legislation, and bureaucrats may do their best to enforce it, but the laws of demand and supply ultimately rule the economy.

4

Sex, Booze, and Drugs

Prior to 1914, cocaine was legal in this country; today it is not. Alcohol (of the intoxicating variety) is legal in United States today; from 1920 to 1933 it was not. Prostitution is legal in Nevada today; in the other 49 states it is not.[1] All of these goods—sex, booze, and drugs—have at least one thing in common: The consumption of each brings together a willing seller with a willing buyer; there is an act of "mutually beneficial exchange" (at least in the opinion of the parties involved). Partly because of this property, attempts to proscribe the consumption of these goods have (1) met with less than spectacular success, and (2) yielded some peculiar patterns of production, distribution, and usage. Let's see why.

When the government seeks to prevent voluntary exchange, it generally must decide whether to go after the seller or the buyer. In most cases—and certainly when sex, booze, or drugs have been involved—the government targets sellers, because this is where the authorities get the most benefit from their enforcement dollars. A cocaine dealer, even a small retail pusher, often supplies dozens or even hundreds of users each day, as did "speakeasies" (illegal saloons) during Prohibition; a hooker typically services anywhere from 3 to 10 "tricks" per day. By incarcerating the supplier, the police can prevent several—or even several hundred—transactions from taking place, which is usually much more cost-effective than going after the buyers one by one. It is not that the police ignore the consumers of illegal goods; indeed, "sting" operations—in which the police pose as illicit sellers—often make the headlines.

---

[1] These statements are not quite correct. Even today, cocaine may be legally obtained by prescription from a physician. Prostitution in Nevada is legal only in those counties that have, by virtue of "local option," chosen to proclaim it as such. Finally, some counties in the United States remain "dry," prohibiting the sale of beer, wine, and distilled spirits.

Nevertheless, most enforcement efforts focus on the supply side, and so shall we.

Law enforcement activities directed against the suppliers of illegal goods increase the suppliers' operating costs. The risks of fines, jail sentences, and possibly even violence become part of the costs of doing business and must be taken into account by existing and potential suppliers. Some entrepreneurs will leave the business, turning their talents to other activities; others will resort to clandestine (and costly) means to hide their operations from the police; still others will restrict the circle of buyers with whom they are willing to deal to minimize the chances that a customer is a cop. Across the board, the costs of operation are higher, and at any given price, less of the product will be available. There is a reduction in supply, and the result is a higher price for the good.

This increase in price is, in a sense, exactly what the enforcement officials are after, for the consumers of sex, booze, and drugs behave according to the law of demand: The higher the price of a good, the lower the amount consumed. So the immediate impact of the enforcement efforts against sellers is to reduce the consumption of the illegal good by buyers. There are, however, some other effects.

First, because the good in question is illegal, people who have a **comparative advantage** in conducting illegal activities will be attracted to the business of supplying (and perhaps demanding) the good. Some may have an existing criminal record and are relatively unconcerned about adding to it. Others may have developed skills in evading detection and prosecution while engaged in other criminal activities. Some may simply look at the illegal activity as another means of thumbing their noses at society. The general point is that when an activity is made illegal, people who are good at being criminals are attracted to that activity.

Illegal contracts usually are not enforceable through legal channels (and even if they were, few suppliers of illegal goods would be stupid enough to complain to the police about not being paid for their products). Thus, buyers and sellers of illegal goods frequently must resort to private methods of contract enforcement—which often means violence.[2] Hence, people who are relatively good at vio-

---

[2] Fundamentally, violence—such as involuntary incarceration—also plays a key role in the government's enforcement of legal contracts. We often do not think of it as violence, of course, because it is usually cushioned by constitutional safeguards, procedural rules, and so on.

lence are attracted to illegal activities, and are given greater incentives to employ their talents. This is one reason why the murder rate in America rose to record levels during Prohibition (1920–1933) and then dropped sharply when liquor was again made legal. It also helps explain why the number of drug-related murders soared during the 1980s, and why "drive-by" shootings became commonplace in many drug-infested cities. The Thompson submachine gun of the 1930s and the MAC-10 machine gun of the 1980s were, importantly, just low-cost means of contract enforcement.

The attempts of law enforcement officials to drive sellers of illegal goods out of business has another effect. Based on recent wholesale prices, $50,000 worth of pure heroin weighs about 4 ounces; $50,000 worth of marijuana weighs about 20 pounds. As any drug smuggler can tell you, hiding 4 ounces of contraband is a lot easier than hiding 20 pounds. Thus, to avoid detection and prosecution, suppliers of the illegal good have an incentive to deal in the more valuable versions of their product, which for drugs and booze means the more potent versions. Bootleggers during Prohibition concentrated on hard liquor rather than beer and wine; even today, "moonshine" typically has roughly twice the alcohol content of legal hard liquor such as bourbon, scotch, or vodka. After narcotics became illegal in this country in 1914, importers switched from the milder opium to its more valuable, more potent, and more addictive derivative, heroin.

The move to the more potent versions of illegal commodities is enhanced by enforcement activities directed against users. Not only do users, like suppliers, find it easier (cheaper) to hide the more potent versions; there is also a change in relative prices due to user penalties. Typically, the law has lower penalties for using an illegal substance than for distributing it. Within each category (use or sale), however, there is commonly the same penalty regardless of value per unit. For example, during Prohibition, a bottle of wine and a bottle of more expensive, more potent hard liquor were equally illegal. Today, the possession of one gram of 90 percent pure cocaine brings the same penalty as the possession of one gram of 10 percent pure cocaine. Given the physical quantities, there is a fixed cost (the legal penalty) associated with being caught, regardless of value per unit (and thus potency) of the substance. Hence, the structure of legal penalties raises the relative price of less potent versions, encouraging users to substitute more potent versions—heroin instead of opium, hashish instead of marijuana, hard liquor instead of beer.

Penalties against users also encourage a change in the nature of usage. Prior to 1914, cocaine was legal in this country and was used openly as a mild stimulant, much as people today use caffeine. (Cocaine was even included in the original formulation of Coca-Cola.) This type of usage—small, regular doses over long time intervals—becomes relatively more expensive when the substance is made illegal. "Extensive" usage (small doses spread over time) is more likely to be detected by the authorities than is "intensive" usage (a large dose consumed at once), simply because possession time is longer and the drug must be accessed more frequently. Thus, when a substance is made illegal, there is an incentive for consumers to switch toward usage that is more intensive. Rather than ingesting cocaine orally in the form of a highly diluted liquid solution, as was commonly done before 1914, people switched to snorting or even injecting it. During Prohibition, people dispensed with cocktails before dinner each night; instead, on the less frequent occasions when they drank, they more often drank to get drunk. The same phenomenon is observed today. People under the age of 21 consume alcoholic beverages less frequently than do people over the age of 21. But when they do drink, they are more likely to drink to get drunk.

Not surprisingly, the suppliers of illegal commodities are reluctant to advertise their wares openly; the police are as capable of reading billboards and watching TV as are potential customers. Suppliers are also reluctant to establish easily recognized identities and regular places and hours of business, because to do so raises the chance of being caught by the police. Information about the price and quality of products being sold goes "underground," often with unfortunate effects for consumers.

With legal goods, consumers have several means of obtaining information. They can learn from friends, from advertisements, and from personal experience. When goods are legal, they can be trademarked for identification. The trademark may not legally be copied, and the courts protect it. Given such easily identified brands, consumers can be made aware of the quality and price of each via the recommendations of friends and advertisements. If their experience does not meet their expectations, they can assure themselves of no further encounter with the unsatisfactory product by never buying that brand again.

When a general class of products becomes illegal, there are fewer ways to obtain information. Brand names are no longer protected by law, so falsification of well-known brands ensues. When products do not meet expectations, it is more difficult (costly) for consumers to punish suppliers. Frequently, the result is degradation of and uncertainty about product quality. The consequences for consumers of the illegal goods are often unpleasant, sometimes fatal.

Consider prostitution. In those counties in Nevada where prostitution is legal, the prostitutes are required to register with the local authorities, and they generally conduct their business within the confines of well-established bordellos. These establishments advertise openly and rely heavily on repeat business. Health officials test the prostitutes weekly for venereal disease and every month for AIDS. Contrast this with other areas of the country, where prostitution is illegal. Suppliers generally are streetwalkers, because a fixed, physical location is too easy for the police to detect and raid. Suppliers change locations frequently, to reduce harassment by police. Repeat business is reported to be minimal; frequently, customers have never seen the prostitute before and will never again.

The difference in outcomes is striking. In Nevada, the spread of venereal disease by legal prostitutes is estimated to be "almost nonexistent"; to date, none of the 9000 registered prostitutes in Nevada has tested positive for AIDS. By contrast, in some major cities outside Nevada the incidence of venereal disease among prostitutes is estimated to be near 100 percent. In Miami, one study found that 19 percent of all incarcerated prostitutes tested positive for AIDS; in Newark, New Jersey, 52 percent of the prostitutes tested were infected with the AIDS virus, and about half of the prostitutes in Washington, D.C., and New York City are also believed to be carrying the AIDS virus. Because of the lack of reliable information in markets for illegal goods, customers frequently do not know exactly what they are getting; as a result, they sometimes get more than they bargained for.

Consider alcohol and drugs. Today, alcoholic beverages are heavily advertised to establish their brand names, and are carried by reputable dealers. Customers can readily punish suppliers for any deviation from the expected potency or quality by withdrawing their business, telling their friends, or even bringing a lawsuit. Similar circumstances prevailed before 1914 in this country for the hundreds of products containing opium or cocaine.

During Prohibition, consumers of alcohol often did not know exactly what they were buying or where to find the supplier the next day if they were dissatisfied. Fly-by-night operators sometimes adulterated liquor with methyl alcohol. In extremely small concentrations, this made watered-down booze taste like it had more "kick"; in only slightly higher concentrations, the methyl alcohol blinded or even killed the unsuspecting consumer. Even in "reputable" speakeasies (those likely to be in business at the same location the next day), bottles bearing the labels of high-priced foreign whiskeys were refilled repeatedly with locally (and illegally) produced "rotgut" until their labels wore off.

In the 1970s, more than one purchaser of what was reputed to be high-potency Panama Red or Acapulco Gold marijuana ended up with low-potency pot heavily loaded with stems, seeds, and maybe even oregano. Buyers of cocaine must worry about not only how much the product has been "cut" along the distribution chain, but also what has been used to cut it. In recent years the purity of cocaine at the retail level has ranged between 10 percent and 95 percent; for heroin, the degree of purity has ranged from 5 percent to 50 percent. Cutting agents can turn out to be any of various sugars, local anesthetics, or amphetamines; on occasion, rat poison has been used.

We noted earlier that the legal penalties for the users of illegal goods encourage them to use more potent forms and to use them more intensively. These facts and the uncertain quality and potency of the illegal products yield a deadly combination. During Prohibition, the death rate from acute alcohol poisoning (i.e., due to an overdose) was more than 30 times higher than today. During 1927 alone, 12,000 people died from acute alcohol poisoning, and many thousands more were blinded or killed by contaminated booze. Today, about 3000 people per year die as a direct result of consuming either cocaine or heroin. Of that total, it is estimated, roughly 80 percent die from (1) an overdose caused by unexpectedly potent product, or (2) an adverse reaction to the material used to cut the drug. Clearly, *caveat emptor* (let the buyer beware) is a warning to be taken seriously if one is consuming an illegal product.

We noted at the beginning of the chapter that one of the effects of making a good illegal is to raise its price. One might well ask, by how much? During the early 1990s, the federal government was spending about $2 billion a year in its efforts to stop the importation of cocaine from Colombia. One recent study concluded that these efforts had hiked the price of cocaine by 4 percent (yes, 4 percent) relative to what it would have been had the federal government done nothing to interdict cocaine imports. The study estimated that the cost of raising the price of cocaine an additional 2 percent would be $1 billion per year.[3]

The government's efforts to halt imports of marijuana have been more successful, presumably because that product is easier to detect than cocaine. Nevertheless, suppliers have responded by cultivating marijuana domestically instead of importing it. The net effect has been an estimated tenfold increase in potency due to the superior farming techniques available in this country.[4]

We might also consider the government's efforts to eliminate the consumption of alcohol during the 1920s and 1930s. They failed so badly that the Eighteenth Amendment, which put Prohibition in place, was the first (and thus far the only) constitutional amendment ever to be repealed. As for prostitution, well, it is reputed to be "the oldest profession," and by all accounts continues flourishing today, even in Newark and Miami.

The government's inability to halt the consumption of sex, booze, or drugs does not in and of itself mean that those efforts have failed. Indeed, the "successes" of these efforts are manifested in their consequences—ranging from tainted drugs and alcohol to disease-ridden prostitutes. The message instead is that when the

---

[3] Federal attempts to prevent cocaine from entering the country are, of course, supplemented by other federal, as well as state and local, efforts to eradicate the drug once it has crossed our borders. To date, there are no empirical estimates of the extent to which these other efforts have increased prices.

[4] There are even reliable reports that some growers in the United States are now using genetic bioengineering to improve their strains. In effect, the government's (partially) successful efforts to stop the importation of marijuana have resulted in technological improvements in marijuana cultivation.

government attempts to prevent mutually beneficial exchange, even its best efforts are unlikely to meet with spectacular success.

DISCUSSION QUESTIONS

1. The federal government currently taxes alcohol on the basis of the "100 proof gallon." (One-hundred-proof alcohol is exactly 50 percent pure ethyl alcohol; most hard liquor sold is 80 proof, or 40 percent ethyl alcohol, whereas wine is usually about 24 proof and most beer is 6–10 proof.) How would alcohol consumption patterns be different if the government taxed alcohol strictly on the basis of volume, rather than taking into account its potency as well?

2. During Prohibition, some speakeasy operators paid bribes to ensure that the police did not raid them. Would you expect the quality of the liquor served in such speakeasies to be higher or lower than in speakeasies that did not pay such bribes? Would you expect any systematic differences (e.g., with regard to income levels) among the customers patronizing the two types of speakeasies?

3. When comparing the markets for prostitution in Nevada and New Jersey, there are two important differences: (1) Prostitutes in New Jersey face higher costs because of government efforts to prosecute them; and (2) customers in New Jersey face higher risks of contracting diseases from prostitutes, because the illegal nature of the business makes reliable information about product quality much more costly to obtain. Given these facts, would you expect the price of prostitution services to be higher or lower in New Jersey, compared to Nevada? Which state would have the higher amount of services consumed (adjusted for population differences)?

4. According to the Surgeon General of the United States, nicotine is the most addictive drug known to humanity, and cigarette smoking kills perhaps 300,000 to 400,000 people per year in the United States. Why isn't tobacco illegal in the United States?

5

Is Water Different?

Mono Lake has gotten a reprieve. Over a 50-year period, this California lake—our country's oldest lake, and one of its most beautiful—shrank from more than 80 square miles in area to about 60. Why? Because in 1941, most of the eastern Sierra mountain water that once fed Mono Lake began disappearing down a 275-mile-long aqueduct, south to Los Angeles, where it was used to wash cars, sprinkle lawns, and otherwise lubricate the lifestyle of southern California. Environmentalists cried out that the diversion of water from Mono Lake must stop. Los Angelenos, who pay $250 per acre-foot for the water, claimed there were no viable alternative sources. Central California farmers, who pay but $10 per acre-foot for subsidized water from the western side of the Sierras, feared that diverting their own "liquid gold" to save Mono Lake would dry up their livelihood. Meanwhile, this migratory rest stop for hundreds of thousands of birds was disappearing.

Finally, in 1994, prodded by the California Water Resources Control Board, and aided by special funds voted by the state legislature, the City of Los Angeles agreed to drastically curtail its usage of Mono Lake water. Under the water-trading plan agreed to, Los Angeles will cut its usage of Mono Lake water by more than 80 percent until the lake's water level has risen 16 feet. Even after that elevation has been reached, the city will limit its usage of Mono Lake water to less than half of its long term average usage. To replace the water it is losing, Los Angeles will buy water from elsewhere, using state funds appropriated for this purpose.

The issues that have arisen over the future of Mono Lake are surfacing in hundreds of locations throughout the United States. Conservationists are increasingly concerned about the toxic contamination of our water supply and the depletion of our underground water sources. Extensive irrigation projects in the western states use more than 150 *billion* gallons of water a day—7 times as much water as all the nation's city water systems combined. The Ogallala aquifer (a 20-million-acre lake beneath the beef-and-breadbasket states of Colorado, Kansas, Nebraska, New Mexico, Oklahoma, and Texas) has been dropping by 3 feet per year because 150,000 wells are pumping water out faster than nature can replenish it.

The common view of water is that it is an overused, precious resource, and that we are running out of it. The economic analysis of the water "problem," however, is not quite so pessimistic, nor so tied to the physical quantities of water that exist on our earth and in the atmosphere. Rather, an economic analysis of water is similar to an analysis of any other scarce resource, revealing that water is fundamentally no different from other scarce resources.

The water industry is one of the oldest and largest in the United States, and the philosophy surrounding it merits some analysis. Many commentators believe that water is unique, that it should not be treated as an **economic good,** that is, a scarce good. Engineering studies that concern themselves with demand for residential water typically use a "requirements" approach. The forecaster simply predicts population changes and then multiplies those estimates by currently available data showing the average amount of water used per person. The underlying assumption of such a forecast is that, regardless of the price charged for water in the future, the same quantity will be demanded per person. Implicitly, then, both the short- and long-run price elasticities of demand are assumed to be zero.

But is this really the case? Perhaps not. Consider, for example, the cities of Tucson and Phoenix in Arizona. Although these cities are located only 100 miles apart, their water-usage rates are notably different. While the average household in Phoenix uses 260 gallons per day, in Tucson the average usage is only 160 gallons per day. Could this usage difference be accounted for by the fact that the price of water is only about half as much per gallon in Phoenix as it is in Tucson? To see why such an influence is likely correct, let's look at a study of water prices in Boulder, Colorado, conducted by economist Steve Hanke.

Boulder was selected by Hanke because a number of years ago the water utility in Boulder installed water meters in every home and business that it supplied. Prior to that time, Boulder, like many other municipalities in the United States, had charged a flat monthly rate for water. Each household paid a specified amount per month no matter how much (or how little) water was used. In essence, the previous flat fee system meant that a zero price was being charged at the margin (for any incremental use of water). The introduction of usage meters meant that a positive price for the marginal unit of water was now imposed.

Hanke looked at the quantity of water demanded both before and after the meters were installed in Boulder. He began by computing an index of water usage, relative to what he called the "ideal" use of water. (The term *ideal* implies nothing from an economic point of view. It merely indicates the minimum quantity of water required to maintain the aesthetic quality of each resident's lawn, taking into account such factors as average temperature, the effect of rainfall, and so forth.) An index value of 100 meant that usage was exactly equal to the hypothetical ideal. A value of, say, 150 meant that residents were using 50 percent more than the ideal, while an index of 75 meant that usage was 25 percent less than Hanke's ideal figure of 100.

From the data in Table 5–1, which compares water usage in Boulder with and without metering, we find that individuals used much more water under the flat-rate system than they did under the metered-rate system. Column 1 shows the meter route numbers of the eight routes studied by Hanke. Column 2 shows the index of water usage for each of the routes during the unmetered period when

TABLE 5–1   Comparing Water Usage With and Without Metering of Actual Usage

(1) Meter Routes	(2) Index of Water Usage (Flat-Rate Period)	(3) Index of Water Usage (Metered-Rate Period)
1	128	78
2	175	72
3	156	72
4	177	63
5	175	97
6	175	102
7	176	105
8	157	86

Source: Adapted from Steve Hanke, "Demand for Water Under Dynamic Conditions," *Water Resources Research*, vol. 6, no. 5, October 1970.

a flat-rate was charged for water usage. The data in Column 3 show water usage on each route for the one-year period after the metering system was put into effect. Note that under the flat rate system every route used substantially more than the ideal amount of water, while under the metered system six of the eight routes used less than the hypothetical ideal. Moreover, water usage dropped substantially on every route when metering was introduced and each user was being charged for the actual amount of water used. Because less water is used in the presence of metering (which raises the price of incremental water), Hanke's data indicate that the quantity of water demanded is a function of the price charged for water. Moreover, Hanke found that for many years after the imposition of the metered-rate pricing system for water, the quantity of water demanded not only remained at a lower level than before metering, but continued to fall slightly. That, of course, means that the long-run **price elasticity of demand** for water was greater than the short-run price elasticity of demand.

Would attaching a dollar sign to water help to solve problems of recurring water **shortages** and endemic waste? Many economists feel it would. It is well known, for example, that much of the water supplied by federal irrigation projects is wasted by farmers and other users because they have no incentive to conserve water and curb overconsumption. The federal government, which has subsidized water projects since 1902, allots water to certain districts, communities, or farmers on the basis of previous usage "requirements." This means that if farmers in a certain irrigation district were to conserve on water usage by, say, upgrading their irrigation systems, their water allotment eventually would be reduced. As a result, a "use it or lose it" attitude has prevailed among users of federal water. Water supplied by federal water projects is also inexpensive. The Congressional Budget Office has estimated that users pay only about 19 percent of the total cost of the water they get.

Economists have suggested that raising the price of federal water would lead to more efficient and less wasteful water consumption. For example, a study by B. Delworth Gardner, an economist now at Brigham Young University, concluded that a 10 percent rise in prices could reduce water use on some California farm crops by as much as 20 percent. Support for such a price increase is politically difficult, however, because federal law stipulates that ability to pay, as well as cost, must be considered when determining water prices.

An alternative solution involving the trading and sale of water rights held by existing federal water users has been proposed by some economists. Such a solution, it is felt, would benefit the economy overall because it could help curb water waste, prevent water shortages, and lessen the need for costly new water projects. Trading and sales of water rights have already taken place in California, Oregon, and Utah. And environmentalists were instrumental in helping arrange the water trading plan for Mono Lake. Despite these modest successes, numerous federal and state laws have, to date, made such trading very difficult.

Until recent years, it had been thought that there was so much water we simply did not have to worry about it—there was always another river or another well to draw on if we ran short. Putting a price tag on water would require a substantial change in the way we have traditionally thought about water. Is this possible or even desirable? Our guess is that the birds of Mono Lake—beneficiaries of the water-trading plan agreed to in 1994—would say Yes.

DISCUSSION QUESTIONS

1. In your opinion, do the data presented in Table 5–1 refute the "water is different" philosophy?
2. How much water does your neighbor "need"? Is your answer the same if you have to pay your neighbor's water bill?
3. Evaluate the following: "Although taxpayers foot the bill for federal water sold to farmers at subsidized prices, they also eat the crops grown with that water. Because the crops are cheaper due to the subsidized water, taxpayers get back exactly what they put in, and so there is no waste from having subsidized water for farmers." Would you give the author of this quote an A or an F in economics?
4. During the drought that plagued California in the late 1980s and early 1990s, farmers in California were able to purchase subsidized water to irrigate their crops, even though many California homeowners had to pay large fines if they watered their lawns. Can you suggest an explanation for this difference in the treatment of two different groups of citizens within the state of California?

6

Rationing Health Care

Americans spend a larger share of national income on health care—more than 14 percent—than any other people of the world. Moreover, for almost every one of the last 20 years, the price index for medical care has increased more rapidly than the price index for all goods and services in general. With spending on health care at record high levels, it is little wonder that some political leaders have labeled health care in the United States a "crisis." The national debate reached a fever pitch in 1994 because President Bill Clinton had made government-mandated, universal health care coverage one of the pillars of his legislative program. While no legislation was passed in that year, the debate lingers on. It is instructive to look at what has happened in other countries that have adopted some form of a national health care system.

We obviously cannot cover every aspect of health care here, nor can we demonstrate that one system of health care delivery is "better" than another one. What we can do, however, is to note the consequences of this critical point: In a world of scarcity, some form of rationing is inevitable. In the market system, that rationing is done by prices. Under the systems of government-mandated, universal health care that now exist (or are likely to exist in the future), prices are not permitted to ration demands. Instead, these systems rely on another system of rationing: It is called "rationing by waiting," because people are forced to wait—for weeks or months—for whatever level of medical care that is offered them.

The most common form of government–mandated, universal health care coverage found in the world today are single-payer health care systems that in essence offer "free" universal health care. (The term "single-payer" arises because the government writes the checks for the medical bills.) Britain offers a typical example. The British National Health Service (NHS) has been in existence since 1948. Once touted as one of the world's best national health care examples, the NHS has deteriorated dramatically. Consider hospital beds: In 1948 there were ten hospital beds per thousand people. Today there are about five per thousand people. Since 1948 about 50 percent of Britain's hospitals have been closed for "efficiency" reasons—meaning that the British government cannot or will not afford to keep them open. Britain now has fewer hospital beds per capita than in every Western European country except Portugal and Spain. Even the two most preeminent teaching hospitals in Britain are scheduled for closure.

Because patients in Britain do not pay directly for the services they receive, some other means of rationing must be used. In Britain, the rationing device is waiting, and as the number of hospital beds and other medical facilities have been cut relative to the population, it is little surprise that waiting times have increased. Currently more than a million British patients are waiting for hospital admission. Many others do not show up on waiting lists because they simply do not apply, knowing that the wait is so long. In some London hospitals, individuals routinely spend more than 12 hours waiting to see a physician.

The total staff in the NHS has, in contrast, skyrocketed. Whereas in 1948 the staff-to-bed ratio was .73 to 1 for each hospital bed, today it is 3.1 to 1 for each hospital bed; even with the drop in beds per capita, there are now twice as many staff members for each patient as there were in 1948. One would expect that this would enhance medical care. Unfortunately, however, the staff, for the most part, do not deal directly with the treatment of patients. Rather, they have become part of the NHS bureaucracy. This is because the government-run NHS adds a new department or committee for every new aspect of medicine that develops. The NHS consists of a bureaucratic network unknown in the decentralized medical system in the United States.

The national health care system in Canada offers another example. In essence, under the Canadian system the government picks up the entire tab for all covered medical procedures. Currently, only 11 percent of Canada's national health care spending goes to administration, compared to 24 percent in the United States. Canada devotes 9.5 percent of its national income to health care, about a third less than in the United States. Perhaps because of the seemingly low cost of the Canadian system, many supporters of health care reform in the United States often point to Canada's system as one that the United States should emulate.

One impact of the lower level of spending in Canada is that their system does not provide the latest in medical technology. For example, compared to the United States, on a per capita basis they have far fewer CAT scan and magnetic resonance imaging (MRI) machines, critical in performing sophisticated, difficult diagnostics. Similarly, Canadian medical facilities have almost none of the medical devices needed to remove kidney stones without painful and dangerous surgery. Moreover, operating rooms in Canada operate on strict financial budgets, and are allowed to continue operating only if they are within those monthly budgets. And what happens if an operating room exhausts its budget on, say, the 20th of the month? It shuts down until the beginning of the next monthly budget cycle.

The costs to the users of the Canadian system show up in other ways as well. Two Canadian economists, Cynthia Ramsay and Michael Walker of the Fraser Institute in British Columbia, have studied the waiting times across a variety of medical specialties. They discovered that many Canadians each year were not permitted to enter the hospital when they or their physician deemed best; instead they had to wait until facilities became available. Moreover, Canadians typically were not even able to get in to see their doctors when they wanted. Ramsay and Walker measured the delay from the time that a primary care physician referred a patient until a specialist actually treated the patient; they found that the demand for health care was rationed by waiting. Listed in Table 6–1 on the next page are the average waiting times in weeks for the services of various medical specialists. The three columns show the waiting times for Canada as a whole and the waiting times in individual Canadian provinces that had, respectively, the shortest and longest waiting times.

Two facts are apparent from Table 6–1. First, it is commonplace for Canadians to have to wait three or four months to receive health care that is anything beyond that offered by a nurse or primary care physician. Second, the Canadian system produces huge inequalities in the way people are treated, not only across illnesses, but also across provinces for the same illness. These long waits, and the ex-

TABLE 6–1   Average Waiting Time for Treatment by a Specialist in Canada

Specialty	Shortest Wait	Longest Wait	Canada Average
		(In Weeks)	
Orthopedics	10.3	39.7	25
Plastic Surgery	9.1	40.5	19.8
Ophthalmology	8.1	39	22.3
Gynecology	5.5	27.2	13.1
Otolaryngology	8.3	26	14.4
Urology	8.2	29.2	12.6
Neurosurgery	10	31	17
General Surgery	6.2	22.3	9.2
Internal Medicine	4.6	7.2	6.4
Cardiovascular	12.5	31.5	17.9

Source: The Fraser Institute, Vancouver, BC, Canada.

tent of unequal treatment, have produced a regular stream of Canadians who come to the United States and spend their own money for medical care here, rather than await their fate at home. It is ironic, but perhaps not surprising, that during America's national debate about health care reform, at least one major Canadian newspaper ran an editorial suggesting that American-style health maintenance organizations (HMOs) might be a solution to Canada's health care problems.

Another example of government-controlled health care involves the Netherlands. The government there decides on global budgets to control hospital expenditures. It also limits the number of doctors who may specialize in a given area and caps the number of patients they may see. In addition, the government controls physician fees. To help the government meet its budgets, many medical specialists have simply stopped working as much as they used to work. It is commonplace for highly trained surgeons to work only half days, or to take weeks off at the end of the year. The result is that currently there is about a three-month waiting list for coronary bypass surgery. Over 15 percent of the patients on the waiting list die before the operation can be performed. Diabetics wait an average of three months to obtain laser treatment for retinal hemorrhaging—and risk blindness in the process. The average wait for removal of gallbladder stones and repairs of hernias is from four to eight weeks. Some forms of reconstructive surgery require waits of up to four years.

Under Dutch law, companies must pay employees' salaries for the first two to six weeks of an illness, depending on the size of the company. This has generated an interesting incentive: The companies have discovered that they can reduce their costs by renting hospital rooms that they keep open for their employees. The companies thus do not have to pay employee salaries while they wait—disabled—for treatment. Although the Dutch system is supposed to provide equal treatment for all, treatment in fact has come to depend on the size and influence of the company for which a person works.

Although our analyses have involved three foreign countries, we need go no further than our own Veterans Administration (VA) to find similar examples of what happens when consumers don't directly pay for what they receive, and producers are not directly rewarded for what they produce. The Veterans Administration operates a 100 percent government-owned and financed health care system. It is the largest health care system in our country and one of the largest in the world. It has 171 medical centers with over 80,000 beds. It operates 362 outpatient and community clinics that receive 23 million patient visits a year. In addition, it has 128 nursing homes with over 70,000 patients. All of the states, plus the District of Columbia and Puerto Rico, have at least one VA medical center, and the VA boasts almost 250,000 employees nationwide.

The General Accounting Office (GAO) did a study of the VA a few years ago, concluding that the VA system faces a growing demand for "free" medical services. Herein lies the rub—the quantity demanded of most services at a zero price will almost always exceed the quantity supplied. Consequently, because price is not used as a rationing device, some other method must be used to ration the scarce resources. Fifty-five percent of the patients who use the VA for routine medical problems wait three hours or longer and sometimes an entire day in order to be seen for a few minutes by a VA general physician. Even among patients requiring urgent medical care, one in nine must wait at least three hours. Patients in need of specialized care cannot even be *seen* by a specialist for 60 to 90 days. They wait months more if surgery or other special procedures are required.

Whether the location is Britain, Canada, Holland, or even the Veterans Administration, when prices are prevented from clearing the market for medical care, waiting time is the most commonly used means of rationing demand. As one unidentified U.S. veteran told the GAO, "I pack a lunch and take a book." Another veteran, retired 69-year-old Army major Elmer Erickson stated, "Be prepared to spend the day there. You will eventually see a doctor."

DISCUSSION QUESTIONS

1. Suppose we had government-mandated universal access to food. How would the outcome likely differ from what is observed with health care systems of this type?
2. Under the Canadian system, those Canadians who are dissatisfied with the health care they receive can come to the United States for medical care if they can afford it. If the United States adopted a system similar to Canada's, where could Americans go if they were not satisfied with the medical care they were receiving?
3. Under the current U.S. health care system, insurance companies often perform the role performed by government agencies under the British, Canadian, and Dutch systems—they pay the bills and they limit the care that people are able to consume. Why might health insurance companies be expected to do a better job in performing these functions?
4. How much health care do people "need." Does this amount depend on the cost of providing it?

7

Choice and Life

The Supreme Court is back in the abortion business. For 16 years, the Court refused to tamper substantively with its 1973 *Roe v. Wade* decision legalizing abortion. But in 1989, in *Webster v. Reproductive Health Services*, the Court upheld the constitutionality of a Missouri law restricting a woman's right to have an abortion.[1] Then, in a 1992 case, *Planned Parenthood v. Casey,* the Supreme Court upheld most of a Pennsylvania law that discourages, but does not prohibit, abortion. Separately, the Court announced its intention to hear other abortion cases posing even more fundamental issues. Since the *Webster* decision, citizens on both sides of the abortion issue have engaged in legislative battles and sometimes violent public protests over the issue of a woman's right to choose versus a fetus's right to live. Thus far most of the legislative battles have been won by the proponents of legal abortions, but the legal battles and protests continue. Barring an unexpectedly swift and unequivocally sweeping pronouncement on the constitutionality of abortion per se, it seems certain that the Supreme Court will be deciding abortion cases long after you have finished reading this book.

Very few of the major issues of our time are purely economic, and abortion is no exception. Economics cannot answer the question of whether life begins at conception, at 24 weeks, or at birth, nor can economics determine whether abortion should be permitted or proscribed. Economics cannot (as yet) even predict how the Supreme Court may ultimately rule on such issues. What economics can do, however, is demonstrate the striking and sometimes surprising implications of the Court's decisions on abortion—whatever those decisions may be.

---

[1] The Court upheld the constitutionality of Missouri statutes barring the expenditure of public funds on abortion and ordering doctors to perform fetal viability tests on women seeking abortions mid-pregnancy or beyond.

Pregnancy termination has been practiced since ancient times, and any legal bars to abortion seem to have been based on the father's right to his offspring. English common law allowed abortion before quickening (when fetal movement is first evident), and there is some doubt whether abortion even after quickening was considered a crime. The American colonies retained the tradition of English common law until the changeover to state statutes at the adoption of the Constitution. In 1828, New York enacted an antiabortion statute that became a model for most other states. The statute declared that abortion before quickening was a misdemeanor and abortion after quickening, second-degree manslaughter. In the late nineteenth century, the quickening distinction disappeared and the penalties for all abortions were increased.

Except under extreme circumstances (such as to protect the life of the mother), abortion remained illegal in this country until about 1960, when a few states began to ease the conditions under which it was legal to perform an abortion. The gradual process of liberalization that state legislatures seemed to be following was suddenly disrupted in 1973 with the landmark Supreme Court decision in *Roe v. Wade*, which overruled all state laws prohibiting abortion before the last three months of pregnancy. In effect, the Court ruled that a woman's right to an abortion was constitutionally protected except during the last stages of pregnancy. There matters stood until the Supreme Court's 1989 decision in *Webster v. Reproductive Health Services.*[2]

Strictly speaking, the court's decision in *Webster* was narrowly focused; its direct impact has been to permit (but not require) states to restrict the circumstances under which abortion is legal. Although the Webster decision stops far short of overturning *Roe v. Wade,* many observers see it as a step (albeit a small one) in that direction, a step that is likely to be followed in subsequent legislative and Supreme Court decisions. Examination of the market for abortions during the period prior to *Roe v. Wade* will help clarify the economic consequences of the court's decision.

Consider first the factors of cost and risk. During the early 1970s, an illegal but otherwise routine abortion by a reputable

---

[2] This is not to say that all was quiet on the abortion front during this period. Indeed, opponents of abortion made numerous attempts to amend the Constitution to either prohibit abortion or establish that abortion was solely the province of the states. All such attempts failed.

physician in the United States typically cost a minimum of $3500 (in 1996 dollars), and could run $5000 in a major East Coast City.[3] Following *Roe v. Wade,* these prices dropped sharply, and by the time of *Webster*, a routine legal abortion performed during the first 3 months of pregnancy cost only about $350.[4] Prior to the legalization of abortion, more than 350,000 women were admitted annually to American hospitals with complications resulting from abortions, and it is estimated that more than 1000 women per year died from improperly performed pregnancy terminations. Following the Court's 1973 decision, complications and deaths from pregnancy termination dropped sharply. In recent years, it is estimated that significant physical complications occur in less than 1 percent of all legal abortions, and deaths due to legal abortions are virtually unknown. In short, the legalization of abortion was associated with a drastic reduction in both the monetary costs and physical dangers of pregnancy termination. Why was such an association observed?

Let us begin by looking at who might be willing to perform an illegal abortion and the price at which she or he would be willing to perform it. A physician convicted of performing an illegal abortion faced not only criminal prosecution (and the associated costs of a legal defense), but also expulsion from the medical profession and the consequent lifetime loss of license and livelihood. In addition, the doctor may have had to endure ostracism by a community that regarded abortion as a criminal act. In short, the costs to a doctor of such a criminal conviction were enormous, and the greatest portion of the fee for an illegal abortion was simply compensation for bearing this potential cost.

It must be acknowledged, of course, that there were physicians who had strong moral convictions regarding a woman's right to abortion. Some were willing to absorb the risks of performing an illegal abortion at a substantially reduced fee. Nevertheless, such physicians were a small minority and not easy to find. Consequently, most women were faced with the choice between either paying $3500 or more for an abortion, paying $700–900 to an unlicensed abortionist operating under unsanitary conditions, or simply doing

---

[3] All of the dollar amounts mentioned in this chapter are adjusted for **inflation** and expressed in terms of 1996 dollars, for purposes of comparison.

[4] More complicated abortions, performed as late as the fifth or sixth month of pregnancy, cost $1200–1400 if done on an outpatient basis in a clinic, and $1600–2000 if performed in a hospital.

without. For those choosing back-alley abortionists, the consequences could include infection, hospitalization, sterility, or death.

The illegality of abortions, of course, increased the cost both of supplying and obtaining information about them; in turn, this made decisions about whether to have an abortion and who should perform it more difficult, and increased the chances of an undesirable outcome. Information is never free, even in legalized activities, because it costs money to acquaint potential buyers with the location, quality, and price of a good or service. But, as was mentioned in Chapter 4, in the case of an illegal activity the provision of information is even more expensive. Abortionists could not advertise, and the more widely they let their availability be known, the more likely they were to be arrested. While some doctors unwilling to perform abortions did refer patients to other, more willing physicians, the referral was itself illegal and therefore risky. Women seeking an abortionist thus were not able to inform themselves of all of the possibilities without spending large amounts of money and time; and even having done so, many were left facing enormous uncertainty about the best path. Some ended up spending too much money; others exposed themselves to unnecessary risks. Some might even have chosen not to have an abortion had they been fully informed of the potential risks.

The situation confronting women during the years prior to the legalization of abortion can be usefully categorized by considering three examples. Although the settings are stylized, they are representative of the nature of the choices involved and the costs and risks of each.

First, there is a wealthy entertainer who visits a travel agency that arranges a package tour of Japan. Included is round-trip airfare, an essentially risk-free procedure in that country (where abortions are legal), and several days of subsequent sightseeing. The price tag: $7500.

Next, let's look at how a young attorney earning $48,000 per year resolves her dilemma. She goes to her physician, who on the quiet refers her to a doctor willing to perform an illegal abortion in his office for $3000. The expense forces the attorney and her husband to delay the purchase of their first home, but then so would the cost of having the baby. Finally, there is a blue-collar couple making $24,000 a year. Surreptitiously asking around, the wife finds out from an acquaintance that the local barber will do the abortion in a back room for $900—aspirins, but not antibiotics, included.

For the wealthy entertainer, both the risk and the financial burden are negligible; to be sure, the money could have been spent on an expensive bauble, but at least there was a trip to Japan in return. For the young lawyer, the financial burden is considerable; if unpaid law school debts preclude either the physician-performed abortion or the cost of completing the pregnancy, the only alternative is the risk of the back-room abortionist. The blue-collar couple gets the worst of both worlds: The abortionist's fee pushes them over their already-tight budget, and the woman risks hospitalization or worse.

The pattern suggested by these examples was borne out in the years preceding the legalization of abortion. Relatively few women had the resources permitting travel to a foreign country where abortion was both safe and legal, nor did many have access to the information needed to learn about and arrange such an undertaking. Somewhat larger numbers of women had established relationships with physicians who either would perform abortions or could refer them to other, willing doctors; these women had the option of choosing between the higher expense of the physician or the greater risk of the unlicensed abortionist. For many women, however, the lack of readily available information about alternatives, combined with the high costs of a physician-performed abortion, meant that the back-room quack, with the attendant risks, was the only realistic means of terminating a pregnancy.

The statistics for New York City in the early 1960s support this argument: Private hospitals performed abortions on 1 pregnant patient in 250; municipal hospitals, 1 in 10,000. The rate for whites was 5 times that for nonwhites and 30 times that for Puerto Ricans. Lower-income women simply were not having as many abortions performed by qualified physicians in suitable surroundings as were upper-income women; as we noted earlier, the result was hundreds of thousands of abortion-related complications, plus more than 1000 deaths each year.

The legalization of abortion in 1973 brought a relatively swift end to such outcomes. No longer faced with the risk of losing liberty and livelihood, thousands of physicians became willing to perform abortions. Even those who, for moral or religious reasons, were unwilling to terminate pregnancies could refer patients to other physicians without legal risk to themselves. Within a short time, properly equipped abortion clinics were established, and even in states requiring that abortions be performed in hospitals, women found a greatly increased range of options. Legalization thus produced an enormous increase in the supply of pregnancy termination services, which in turn had several consequences.

As in any market in which there is an increase in supply, the price of abortions fell drastically; holding quality and safety constant, the price reduction was as much as 90 percent. The decline in the price of physician-supplied abortions to levels at or below those charged by back-alley abortionists quickly drove most of the quacks out of business. As a result, the safety of abortions increased dramatically; serious infections and deaths due to abortion are estimated to have declined by 50 percent within a year of *Roe v. Wade,* and have since become quite rare. Information about abortions, once available only "on the sly" and at considerable trouble and expense, became openly available. A woman considering pregnancy termination could call her physician's office or simply look in the telephone book for information about local services. Moreover, not only was knowledge about the price, quality, and safety of abortion openly available, so too were counseling services about the potentially adverse psychological or emotional consequences of what, for many women, was a difficult and trying decision.

As would be expected, the lower price of abortion and the more widely available information about the procedure combined to bring about a large increase in the number of abortions performed in this country. During 1973, slightly over 700,000 legal abortions were performed in the United States, many of them in the aftermath of the Supreme Court's landmark decision. One early study concluded that of the legal abortions that took place in the year following *Roe v. Wade,* "well over half—most likely between two-thirds and three-fourths . . . were replacements for illegal abortions."[5] By 1981, 1.6 million legal abortions per year were being performed in the United States, a rate that has risen only slightly since.

What then have been the consequences of the Court's decision in *Webster*? In the short run, not much. To be sure, abortions in public facilities in Missouri are now illegal, and women in the later stages of pregnancy must undergo costly and risky tests regarding fetal viability before having an abortion. Thus the Court's decision has increased the costs of pregnancy termination in Missouri. The result has been fewer abortions, perhaps some illegal abortions, and the selection of more effective means of (pre-pregnancy) birth con-

[5] June Skylar and Beth Berkov, "Abortion, Illegitimacy, and the American Birth Rate," *Science,* vol. 185, September 13, 1974, pp. 914ff.

trol. Nevertheless, there are good (albeit more expensive) substitutes available—abortions in private facilities or in neighboring states—so that the magnitude of these effects has been small. If the Court goes beyond the step it took in *Webster*, and if very many states (successfully) impose additional restrictions on abortion, there will be a more noticeable return to the conditions that prevailed before 1973: Abortions will become more expensive and less frequent, and more of them will be performed illegally and less safely. As was the case before 1973, the burden of these consequences will be borne largely by women in the middle- and lower-income brackets.

We emphasized at the beginning of this chapter that the issues raised by abortion go far beyond the economic consequences, and that economics cannot, in any event, determine whether abortion should be permitted or proscribed. What economics can do—as we hope that we have shown—is to illustrate some of the consequences of the decision between "choice" and "life." Whether an understanding of those consequences can—or even should—play a role in making that decision is a matter we can leave only to the reader.

DISCUSSION QUESTIONS

1. Suppose you wished to predict which states would impose more restrictive conditions on abortions. What factors—for example, per capita income and average age of the population—would you take into account in making your predictions?

2. Before 1973, legal penalties generally were imposed on suppliers of abortion rather than on demanders. How might the effects of prohibiting abortion been different had legal penalties been imposed on demanders rather than on suppliers?

3. The discussion in this chapter focused solely on the economic consequences of prohibiting abortion. Do you think that legislatures base their decisions about abortion solely on the economic consequences? Can an understanding of the economic consequences of laws give us (and legislatures) any guidance about the "best" public policy on abortions?

4. As of 1996, it was up to the states to decide on public policy regarding abortion. Some people have argued that the federal government (perhaps through a Constitutional amendment) should decide on a uniform national policy regarding abortions. What are the advantages and disadvantages of having separate state policies rather than a uniform national policy?

8

Bankrupt Landlords, from Sea to Shining Sea

Take a tour of Santa Monica, a beachfront enclave of Los Angeles, and you will find a city of bizarre contrasts. Pick a street at random and you will likely find run-down rental units sitting in disrepair next to homes costing $500,000. Try another street and you will find abandoned apartment buildings adjacent to luxury car dealerships and trendy shops that sell high-fashion clothing to Hollywood stars. Sound strange? Not in Santa Monica—known locally as the People's Republic of Santa Monica—where stringent rent control laws routinely force property owners to leave their buildings empty and decaying rather than even bothering to sell them.

Three thousand miles to the east, rent control laws in New York City—known locally as the Big Apple—are forcing landlords to *abandon* 2000 housing units per *month* because the owners no longer can afford the financial losses imposed by rent control. Largely as a result of such abandonments, the city government of New York owns more than 150,000 derelict housing units—empty, except for rats and small-time cocaine dealers. Meanwhile, because the controls also discourage new construction, the city faces a "housing gap" of 200,000 rental units—apartments that easily could be filled at current controlled rental rates, if the units existed in habitable form.

From coast to coast, stories like these are commonplace in the 200-plus American cities and towns that practice some form of rent control—a system in which the local government tells building owners how much they can charge for rent. Time and again, the stories are the same: poorly maintained rental units, abandoned apartment buildings, tenants trapped by housing gridlock in apartments no longer suitable for them, bureaucracies bloated with rent control enforcers, and even homeless families that can find *no one* who will rent to them. And time and again, the reason for the stories is the same: legal limits on the rent that people may pay for a place to live.

Our story begins in 1943, when the federal government imposed rent control as a temporary wartime measure. Although the federal program ended after the war, New York City continued the controls on its own. Under New York's controls, a landlord generally could not raise rents on apartments as long as the tenants continued to re-new their leases.[1] Rent controls in Santa Monica are more recent. They were spurred by the inflation of the 1970s, which, combined with California's rapid population growth, pushed housing prices and rents to record levels. In 1979, the city of Santa Monica ordered rents rolled back to their levels of the year before, and stipulated that future rents could go up by only two-thirds as much as any increase in the overall price level. In both New York and Santa Monica, the objective of the controls has been to keep rents below the levels that would be observed in freely competitive markets. Achieving this goal has required that both cities impose extensive regulations to prevent landlord and tenant from evading the controls—regulations that are costly to enforce and that distort the normal operation of the market.

In general, the unfettered movement of rental prices in a freely competitive housing market performs three vital functions: Prices allocate existing scarce housing among competing claimants; they promote the efficient maintenance of existing housing, and stimulate the production of new housing, where appropriate; and they ration usage of housing by demanders, thereby preventing waste of scarce housing. Rent control prevents rental prices from effectively performing these functions. Let's see how.

Rent control discourages the construction of new rental units. Developers and mortgage lenders are reluctant to get involved in building new rental properties because controls artificially depress the most important long-run determinant of profitability—rents.

---

[1] Since 1974, some apartments in New York have been subject only to more flexible "rent stabilization" regulations, rather than to absolute rent controls. The qualitative effects of the two sets of controls are much the same, so we do not emphasize the distinction here.

Thus, in one recent year, 11,000 new housing units were built in Dallas, a city with a 16 percent rental vacancy rate but no rent control statute. In that same year, only 2000 units were built in San Francisco, a city with a 1.6 percent vacancy rate but stringent rent control laws. In New York City, the only rental units being built are either exempt from controls, or are heavily subsidized by the government. Private construction of new apartments in Santa Monica has also dried up, even though new office space and commercial developments—both exempt from rent control—are being built at a record pace.

Rent control leads to the deterioration of the existing supply of rental housing. When rental prices are held below free market levels, property owners cannot recover through higher rents the costs of maintenance, repairs, and capital improvements. Thus, such activities are sharply curtailed. Eventually, taxes, utilities, and the expenses of the most rudimentary repairs—such as replacing broken windows—overwhelm the depressed rental receipts; as a result, the buildings are abandoned. In New York, some owners have resorted to arson, hoping to collect the insurance on their empty rent-controlled buildings before the city claims them for back taxes. In Santa Monica, many owners would like to convert their empty buildings to other uses, but to do so, the city insists that they must pay to build new rental units—at a cost of up to $50,000 per apartment—to replace the units they no longer rent. Not surprisingly, few owners have been willing to bear this burden, so the buildings sit, graffiti-scarred and empty.

Rent control impedes the process of rationing scarce housing. One consequence of this is that tenant mobility is sharply restricted. Even when a family's demand for living space changes—due, for example, to a new baby or a teenager's departure for college—there can be substantial costs in giving up a rent-controlled unit. In both New York City and Santa Monica, landlords often charge "key money" (a large, up-front cash payment) before a new tenant is allowed to move in. The high cost of moving means that large families often stay in cramped quarters while small families, or even single persons, reside in very large units. In New York, this phenomenon of nonmobility has come to be known as "housing gridlock." In Santa Monica, many homeowners rented out portions of their houses in response to soaring prices in the 1970s, and now find themselves trapped by their tenants, whom they cannot evict even if they want to sell their homes and move to a retirement community.

Not surprisingly, the distortions produced by rent control lead to efforts by both landlords and tenants to evade the rules. This in turn leads to the growth of cumbersome and expensive government bureaucracies whose job is to enforce the controls. In New York, where rents can be raised when tenancy changes hands, landlords have an incentive to make life unpleasant for tenants, or to evict them on the slightest pretense. The city has responded by making evictions extremely costly for landlords. Even if a tenant blatantly and repeatedly violates the terms of a lease, the tenant cannot be evicted if the violations are corrected within a "reasonable" time period. If the violations are not corrected—despite several trips to court by the owners and their attorneys—eviction requires a tedious and expensive judicial proceeding. For their part, tenants routinely try to "sublet" all or part of their rent-controlled apartments at prices substantially above the rent they pay the owner. Because both the city and the landlords try to prohibit subletting, the parties often end up in the city's Housing Courts, an entire judicial system developed chiefly to deal with disputes over rent-controlled apartments.

In Santa Monica, tenants can be evicted, but only after the landlord pays them a "relocation fee" of up to $3000. Even then, the landlord cannot hike the rent for a new tenant. It is little wonder that prospective renters often pay key money of $5000 or more to become tenants—when they are lucky enough to find an apartment available. Even so, the strict controls on monthly rents often force landlords to use other means to discriminate among prospective tenants. Simply to ensure that the rent check comes every month, many landlords rent only to well-heeled professionals. As one commentator puts it, "There is no disputing that Santa Monica has become younger, whiter, and richer under rent control." The same pattern has occurred under the rent control laws of both Berkeley, California, and Cambridge, Massachusetts.

There is little doubt the bureaucracies that have evolved to administer rent control laws are cumbersome, expensive, and growing. Between 1988 and 1993 New York City spent $5.1 billion rehabilitating housing confiscated from private landlords. Even so, derelict buildings are piling up at a record rate. The overflow and appeals from the city's Housing Courts are now clogging the rest of New

York's judicial system, impeding the prosecution of violent criminals and drug dealers. In Santa Monica, the Rent Control Board began with an annual budget of $745,000 and a staff of 20 people. By the early 1990s, the staff had tripled in size and the budget was pushing $5 million. And who picks up the tab? The landlords do, of course, with an annual special assessment of $200 per unit levied on them.

Ironically, the big losers from rent control—in addition to landlords—are often low-income individuals, especially single mothers. Indeed, many observers now believe that one significant cause of homelessness in cities such as New York and Los Angeles is rent control. Typically, poor individuals can neither afford a hefty key money payment nor assure the discriminating landlord that their rent will be paid on time—much less paid—each month. Because controlled rents generally are well below free-market levels, there is little incentive for apartment owners to take a chance on low-income individuals as tenants. This is especially true if the prospective tenant's chief source of income is a welfare check. Indeed, a significant number of the tenants appearing in New York's Housing Courts are low-income mothers who, due to emergency expenses or delayed welfare checks, have missed rent payments. Often their appeals end in evictions and new homes in temporary public shelters, or on the streets. In Santa Monica, some owners who used to rent one- and two-room units to welfare recipients and other low-income individuals have simply abandoned their buildings, leaving them vacant rather than try to collect artificially depressed rents that fail to cover operating costs. The disgusted owner of one empty and decaying 18-unit building had a friend spray-paint his feelings on the wall: "I want to tear this mess down, but Big Brother won't let me." Perhaps because the owner had escaped from a concentration camp in search of freedom in the United States, the friend added a personalized touch: a drawing of a large hammer and sickle, symbol of the former Soviet Union.

It is worth noting that the ravages of rent controls are not confined to capitalist nations. In a heavily publicized news conference, the foreign minister of Vietnam, Nguyen Co Thach, recently declared that a "romantic conception of socialism" had destroyed his country's economy after the Vietnam War. Mr. Thach stated that rent control had artificially encouraged demand and discouraged supply, and that all of the housing in Hanoi had fallen into disrepair as a result. Thach concluded by noting, "The Americans couldn't destroy Hanoi, but we have destroyed our city by very low rents. We realized it was stupid and that we must change policy." One can only wonder when the People's Republic of Santa Monica will get the message.

DISCUSSION QUESTIONS

1. Why do you think that governments frequently attempt to control apartment rents but not house prices?
2. What determines the size of the "key money" payments that landlords demand (and tenants offer) for the right to rent a controlled apartment?
3. Who, other than the owners of rental units, loses as a result of rent controls? Who gains from rent controls? What effect would the imposition of rent controls have on the market price of an existing single-family house? What effect would rent controls have on the value of vacant land?
4. Why do the owners of rental units reduce their maintenance expenditures on the units when rent controls are imposed? Does their decision have anything to do with whether or not they can "afford" those expenditures?

Part Three

Market Structures

INTRODUCTION

The competitive model employed in our discussion of demand and supply in Part Two assumes that firms on both sides of the market satisfy the conditions of **pure competition.** For sellers of goods, this means the demand curve each of them faces is **perfectly elastic:** Suppliers must take the market price as given, for any attempt by them to raise price above the market price will result in the loss of all of their sales. Similarly, purchasers in the competitive model face a supply curve that is also perfectly elastic. The market price is given, and any attempt by them to purchase at less than that price will be unsuccessful—no one will sell to them.

The conditions of pure **competition** imply that buyers and sellers have no effect individually on market prices. Even a casual glance at the world suggests that the conditions of pure competition are not always met. Sometimes, as is the case for major corporations, the firms are large enough relative to the market that significant changes in their purchase or sale decisions clearly must have an effect on prices. Other times, buyers or sellers are somehow "unique," in that no other buyer or seller offers exactly what they do. (Classic examples include the superstars of sports (e.g., Shaquille O'Neal) and entertainment (e.g., Madonna), who will sell less of their services if they raise their prices, but will still sell some.) Sometimes firms that otherwise would be pure competitors join together to form a cartel, acting as a single decision-making unit whose collective output decisions affect the market price.

61

When a seller's decisions affect the price of a good, economists usually call the firm a monopoly. Literally, this means "single seller," but what is actually meant is that the firm faces a downward-sloping demand curve for its output, so that its decisions affect the price at which its output is sold. When a buyer's decisions affect the market price, we term the firm a monopsony, or "single buyer." This just means that the firm faces a positively-sloped supply curve, so that its purchasing decisions affect the price at which it buys goods. (Some economists use the term **price searcher** to mean any firm—buyer or seller—whose decisions affect market prices, and who must therefore search for (or decide upon) the price that maximizes the firm's profits. Following this terminology, a pure competitor would be called a **price taker,** for such a firm takes the market price as given.)

The starting point for our examination of different market structures, Chapter 9, "A Random Walk Down Wall Street," provides a look at the ultimate purely competitive market: Wall Street, where stocks and bonds are traded each day. The goods involved in this market are homogeneous, market participants do not seem to care with whom they exchange, and information is transmitted cheaply and quickly. As a result, the conditions for the model of pure competition are met here as well as they are in any market. One of the surprising conclusions we reach is that get-rich schemes that propose to somehow "beat the market" are doomed to failure. Unless you have inside information that is not publicly available, a random selection of stocks and bonds is just as likely to make money as is a portfolio recommended by your stock or bond broker.

If Wall Street provides the ultimate example of capitalist competition, the market for caviar has exemplified—at least until recently—the opposite end of the spectrum: It has been a communist cartel. Beginning shortly after the Bolshevik revolution, the government of the Soviet Union took control of the sources of the world's best caviar and restricted supplies of the good to maximize the profits obtained from caviar sales. As we see in Chapter 10, "The Collapse of the Communist Caviar Cartel," however, trying to keep a cartel together is tough business—so tough that as soon as the iron grip of the central government was released, the cartel collapsed. The overriding message of this chapter is that, although the profit potential of cartels is enormous, competitive pressures make them inherently unstable, and thus generally short-lived.

Although most discussions of monopoly and monopsony focus on private firms, we see in Chapter 11, "Faulty Prices," that governments can get into the act too. Because state governments often determine the rules of the game under which market participants must operate, states can change those rules to benefit (or harm) those participants. This is exactly what several states have done in the market for automobile insurance. Under the guise of insurance "reform," several large states have tried to force suppliers of auto insurance to reduce their premiums (the prices they charge purchasers of insurance). In effect, these state governments are acting like monopsonists. To the extent that the states are successful, those drivers who are able to retain their insurance will benefit from lower premiums. Nevertheless, the mandated reduction in the price of insurance lowers the profits of insurance companies, and will cause them to cancel (or refuse to issue) policies for some drivers. Hence, both the insurance companies and those drivers who are unable to get insurance will be made worse off as a result of the states' actions.

The final pair of chapters in this section examine market structures that are perhaps less conventional than the average market we are likely to encounter. Interestingly, one of them thrives because of government regulations, while the other exists despite government efforts to eliminate it.

In Chapter 12, "Inner City High Finance," we examine why pawnshops and check cashing services have begun flourishing over the past decade, and why their operations are almost exclusively confined to low-income inner cities. The answer, we find, lies in the federal Community Reinvestment Act (CRA), which requires banks to make loans and investments in the areas in which they accept deposits. The CRA was expressly designed to encourage lending that would help rehabilitate America's inner cities. In fact, the law greatly increased the potential lending risks faced by banks that have branches located in low-income areas. As a result, banks have closed branches they used to have in these areas, and refrained from opening ones they might have operated. This has created a market void, into which the pawnshops and check-cashing services have stepped. One important message of this chapter is that even when the market outcome is not perfect, government efforts to alter market outcomes may not always lead to improvement.

If you have ever tried to get a ticket to a popular rock concert or sports event you are likely to be interested in Chapter 13, "Getting Scalped." You probably know that by the time you decide to purchase your tickets, the local official ticket agencies may be sold out. Enter the ticket scalper, who is willing—for a price—to ensure that you can get the tickets you want. From an economist's perspective, ticket scalpers perform the classic role of a middleman: They buy low and sell high. This chapter examines the (productive) role played by ticket scalpers, and why they continue to exist despite the best efforts of some governments to put them out of business.

9

A Random Walk Down Wall Street

Want to get rich quick? We know of only two sure ways:
1. Marry a wealthy person.
2. Buy low and sell high.

Based on the authors' experiences, we cannot help you much with the first method; but we may be able to help you with the second.

Let us begin with the financial pages (sometimes called the business section) of the daily newspaper. There you will find column after column of information about the stocks and bonds of U.S. corporations. A **share of stock** in a corporation is simply a legal claim to a share of the corporation's future profits; owners of stocks are called **shareholders.** Thus, if there are 100,000 shares of stock in a company and you, as a shareholder, own 1000 of them, then you own the right to 1 percent of that company's future profits.

A **bond** is a legal claim against a firm, entitling the bond owner to receive a fixed annual "coupon" payment, plus a lump sum payment at the bond's maturity date. (Coupon payments on bonds get their name from the fact that bonds once had coupons attached to them when issued. Each year, the owner would clip a coupon off the bond and send it to the issuing firm in return for that year's interest.) Bonds are issued in return for funds lent to the firm. The coupon payments represent interest on the amount borrowed by the firm, and the lump sum payment at maturity generally equals the amount originally borrowed. Bonds are *not* claims to the future profits of the firm; legally, the owners of the bonds, called bond-holders, are to be paid whether the firm prospers or not.[1]

Now, suppose that in your quest for riches, you decide to buy some shares of stock in a corporation. How should you choose which corporation's stock to buy? One way is to consult a specialist in stocks, called a **stockbroker.** Such brokers have access to an enormous amount of information. They can tell you what lines of business specific corporations are in, who the firms' major competitors are, how profitable the firms have been in the past, and whether their stocks' prices have risen or fallen. If pressed, they probably will be willing to recommend which stocks to buy. Throughout, any broker's opinion will sound highly informed and authoritative.

Strange as it may seem, though, a broker's investment advice is not likely to be any better than anyone else's. In fact, *the chances of the broker's being right are no greater than the chances of your being right!* On average you are just as likely to get rich by throwing darts at the financial pages of your newspaper. Let's see why.

Some years ago, the editors of the business magazine *Forbes* taped the financial pages of a major newspaper to a wall and threw darts at the portion listing stock prices. They hit the stocks of 28 different companies and invested a hypothetical $1000 in each. When the editors halted their experiment, the original $28,000 had grown to $132,000—a gain of 370 percent. Over the same period, the Dow Jones Industrial Average (a leading measure of the stock market's overall performance) grew less than 40 percent in value. Perhaps even more impressive, Forbes' random selection of stocks outperformed the recommended stock portfolios of most of the "gurus" of stock market forecasting.

More recently, the editors of *The Wall Street Journal,* a major financial newspaper, tried a similar experiment. Each month they invited four stockbrokers to recommend a stock to buy; the four stocks became the "experts' portfolio" for the month. Then the editors threw four darts at the financial pages of their newspaper to select four stocks that became the "darts' portfolio" for the month. Over time, the particular expert brokers changed, depending on

---

[1] To ensure this, bondholders generally must receive their coupon payments each year, plus any principal due, before any shareholders can receive their share of the firm's profits, called dividends.

how well their picks performed relative to the darts' portfolio. Any broker whose stock beat the darts got to pick again the next month. Any expert beaten by the darts was replaced the next month by a new broker. At six-month intervals, the newspaper tallied up the performances of the experts versus the darts. After several years of running the experiment, the general result was this: Although the experts beat the darts over the long haul, the winning margin was tiny. Moreover, there were several six-month periods in which the darts actually *outperformed* the experts. How did the darts do it?

Suppose that you, and you alone, noticed that the price of a particular stock moved in a predictable manner. Specifically, assume the price *rose* 5 percent on even-numbered days and *fell* 5 percent on odd-numbered days, resulting in (approximately) no average change over time. Knowing this fact, how do you make money? You simply buy shares of the stock just before it is due to rise, and sell shares of the stock just before it is due to fall. If you start the year with $1000 and reinvest your profits, following this strategy would yield profits in excess of $500,000 by the end of the year. If you continue this strategy for a second year, your wealth would exceed $250 million!

Of course, as your wealth accumulates—"buying low and selling high"—your purchases and sales would start to affect the price of the stock. In particular, your purchases would drive the low prices up and your sales would drive high prices down. Ultimately, your buying and selling in response to predictable patterns would *eliminate* those patterns, and there would be no profit potential left to exploit. This is *exactly* what happens in the stock market—except it happens far faster than a single person could accomplish it alone.

At any point in time, there are tens of thousands, perhaps millions, of persons looking for any bit of information that will help them forecast the future prices of stocks. Responding to any information that seems useful, these people try to "buy low and sell high." As a result, all publicly available information that might be used to forecast stock prices gets taken into account—leaving no

---

[2] See L. J. Feinstone, "Minute by Minute: Efficiency, Normality and Randomness in Intra-Daily Asset Prices," *Journal of Applied Econometric,s* vol. 2, 1987, pp. 193–214.

predictable profits. And, because there are so many people involved in this process, it occurs quite swiftly. Indeed, there is evidence that all information entering the market is fully incorporated into stock prices within *less than a minute* of its arrival.[2]

The result is that stock prices tend to follow a **random walk**— which is to say that the best forecast of tomorrow's price is today's price, plus a random component. Although large values of the random component are less likely than small values, nothing else about its magnitude or sign (positive or negative) can be predicted. Indeed, the random component of stock prices exhibits behavior much like what would occur if you rolled two dice and subtracted seven from the resulting score. *On average,* the dice will total 7, so after you subtract 7, the average result will be zero. It is true that rolling a 12 or a 2 (yielding a net score of +5 or –5) is less likely than rolling an 8 or a 6 (producing a net score of +1 or –1). Nevertheless, positive and negative net scores are equally likely, and the expected net score is zero.[3]

It is worth emphasizing that the bond market operates every bit as efficiently as the stock market. That is, investors in bonds study the available information and use whatever might help them forecast future bond prices. And because they exploit this information up to the point that the benefits of doing so are just matched by the costs, there remains no publicly available information that can profitably be used to improve bond price forecasts. As a result, bond prices, like stock prices, follow a random walk. Moreover, because interest rates are inextricably linked to the prices of bonds, interest rates also follow a random walk.

In light of this discussion, two questions arise. First, are all the efforts put into forecasting stock and bond prices simply a waste? The answer is no. From a social viewpoint, this effort is productive because it helps ensure that asset prices correctly reflect all available information, and thus that resources are allocated efficiently. From a private standpoint, the effort is also rewarding, just as any other productive activity is rewarding. At the margin, the gains from

[3] Strictly speaking, stock prices follow a random walk with "drift"; that is, on average they rise at a real (inflation-adjusted) rate of about 3 percent per year over long periods of time. This drift, which is the average compensation investors receive for deferring consumption, can be thought of as the 7 that comes up on average when two dice are rolled.

trying to forecast future stock and bond prices are exactly equal to the costs; there are no unexploited profit opportunities. Unless you happen to have some unique ability that makes you better than others, you will earn only enough to cover your costs—but of course the same is true of growing wheat or selling women's shoes. So, absent some special ability, you are just as well off investing in the market based on the roll of the dice or the throw of a dart.

The second question is a bit trickier: Isn't there any way to "beat the market"? The answer is yes—but only if you have **inside information**, that is information unavailable to the public. Suppose, for example, that your best friend is in charge of new product development for Mousetrap Inc., a firm that just last night invented a mousetrap superior to all others on the market. No one but your friend—and now you—are aware of this. You could indeed make money with this information, by purchasing shares of Mousetrap Inc. and then selling them (at a higher price) as soon as the invention is publicly announced. There is one problem: Stock trading based on such inside information is illegal, punishable by substantial fines and even imprisonment. Unless you happen to have a stronger-than-average desire for a long vacation in a federal prison, our money-making advice to you is simple: Invest in the mousetrap after it hits the market—and throw darts in the meantime.

DISCUSSION QUESTIONS

1. Why do you think the government prohibits trading on the basis of inside information?

2. Can you think of any other assets whose prices might follow random walks?

3. When the prices of stocks fall, newspapers often report that the decline in prices was caused by a "wave of selling." By the definition of exchange, every sale must be accompanied by a purchase. Why then do the newspapers not report that the decline in stock prices was caused by a "wave of purchasing"?

4. If stockbrokers cannot "beat the market," why do people use their services?

10

The Collapse of the Communist Caviar Cartel

First the Berlin Wall came tumbling down. Then the Soviet Union disintegrated. This, however, is surely the final death knell of communism: The caviar cartel has collapsed. After seven decades of iron rule by the Soviet state, competition in the caviar business has reared its ugly head, and beluga is at risk of becoming as bourgeois as black bread. Caviar prices dropped 20 percent and show signs of heading even lower. How has this sad state of affairs come to pass?

Our story begins in the Volga River Delta, where Kazakhstan and Russia (both former members of the Soviet Union) share a border at the northern end of the Caspian Sea. Both the temperature and salinity of the water in the Delta apparently make it the ideal spawning ground for sturgeon, the long-nosed prehistoric fish whose eggs have for centuries been viewed as the world's finest caviar. When the Russian czars and czarinas ran the show, legend has it that fresh caviar was rushed to Moscow and St. Petersburg on horseback, with fresh ice applied with every change of horses. And there is little doubt that the Russian royalty had quite a taste for elite fish eggs; a description of one royal banquet served in the 1890s reported that the scene was dominated by "huge blocks of the rare pressed caviar. . . which towered over everything else at the table."

Once the Bolsheviks disposed of the Romanovs in 1917, they quickly saw the potential profits to be had from cornering the market on caviar. Thus, for the next 70 years or so, a state-dominated cartel controlled the beluga business from top to bottom, beginning with the harvest, followed by the processing (adding just a dash of salt), and concluding with the packaging and export of the final product. Although the Soviet sturgeon have been considerate enough to produce an annual catch of some 2000 tons of caviar, the communist cartel allowed only 150 tons out of the country. As a result, a state-supplied kilogram (2.2 pounds) of top-grade black caviar costing $5 or less on the Moscow black market, commanded $2000 or more in New York. There is no doubt that Soviet success in restricting the supplies of caviar to capitalist consumers pushed its price far above competitive levels. But how did the communists manage this feat, and what happened to blacken the outlook for the fish egg business?

In general, a cartel must meet four basic requirements if it is to be successful:

1. It must control a large share of actual and potential output, so that other producers of the good it sells will not be able to expand output significantly, thereby depressing prices.

2. Substitutes for the good sold by the cartel must be relatively poor alternatives (as viewed by consumers), few in number, and relatively inelastic in supply; these factors all help reduce the **elasticity of demand** facing the cartel, and thus enable it to raise price.

3. There must be relatively few outside factors that tend to disturb cost or demand conditions in the industry, so that the cartel is not continually having to make new price and output decisions in response to changing conditions; thus, for example, the demand for the industry's product should be relatively insensitive to economic **expansions** and **recessions.**

4. It must be relatively easy for the cartel to identify and punish cartel members who cheat on the cartel agreement by cutting price and expanding output.

Meeting these basic requirements is something that all successful cartels have been able to do to some extent. Just as significantly, it has been a breakdown in one or more of these factors that has been the downfall of each of them.

Until the collapse of the Soviet Union, the communist caviar cartel satisfied all of these conditions, and thus was one of the most successful on record. First, the only other significant producer of Caspian Sea caviar was Iran, and the royal family of Iran, although no friend of communism, was quite happy to enjoy the profits that came from letting the Soviets raise the market price of top-quality caviar. Second, although most fish produce eggs, there seems to be something special about sturgeon eggs that consumers find uniquely tasty, and the Caspian Sea is the only place in the world where sturgeon have been able to survive in great enough numbers to make large-scale harvesting of their eggs economical. Third, the consumers of top-quality caviar tend to be concentrated in the highest of the high- income brackets, where they are largely insulated from the ups and downs of the economy. Fourth, the very nature of the Soviet police state—with informants on every street corner, and no aversion to the use of force against those who broke the rules—made the USSR an ideal location for a cartel, particularly because the government was in charge of the cartel.

Communists, of course, are not the only ones who know how to fix prices. Another hugely successful cartel has been the Organization of Petroleum Exporting Countries (OPEC). Formed in 1960, its members have included such major oil-producing countries as Algeria, Indonesia, Iran, Iraq, Kuwait, Libya, Nigeria, Saudi Arabia, and Venezuela. OPEC had little impact on the price of oil until the early 1970s, but the outbreak of the Middle East war in 1973 provided the impetus for cohesive action. In the wake of the war, Saudi Arabia, Kuwait, and several other Arab nations sharply reduced their production of oil. Because the demand for oil is downward sloping, this reduction in supply pushed oil prices—and thus the profits of OPEC members—up sharply. On January 1, 1973, one could buy Saudi Arabian crude oil at $2.12 per barrel. Within one year, the price of crude had risen to $7.61 per barrel; by 1975, to $10.50; and by the end of the decade, the price of oil was $25 per barrel and rising.

A variety of forces combined to end the success of OPEC—at least for now. At least partly in response to the high prices charged by OPEC, worldwide supplies of oil began to grow, led by rising production on Alaska's North Slope and by aggressive marketing of the oil flowing out of the Norwegian and British fields located in the North Sea. Eventually, this additional output significantly reduced the market share controlled by OPEC members, and helped reduce their stranglehold on price. The worldwide recession of 1981–1982 also battered OPEC, for the decline in consumer incomes and industrial activity reduced the demand for petroleum products and added to the downward pressure on oil prices. In March 1983, for the first time in its 23-year history, OPEC agreed to cut the posted price of its crude oil.

The coup de grâce for OPEC, however, as it is with so many cartels, has been cheating on the cartel agreement by its members. Whenever there are numerous firms or countries in a cartel arrangement, there will always be some that are unhappy with the situation, perhaps because they think they are not getting a large enough share of the profits. They will want to cheat by charging a slightly lower price than the one stipulated by the cartel. Members who are producing a small percentage of the total output of the cartel face a very elastic demand curve if they cheat and no one else does. A small drop in price by a cheater will result in a very large increase in its revenues (and thus profits). The potential for cheating is a constant threat to a cartel's existence, and when enough of a cartel's members try to cheat, the cartel breaks up.

In the case of OPEC, war between the member nations of Iran and Iraq precipitated a major outbreak of cheating as those two nations expanded production beyond their quotas, using the extra sales to finance heavy military expenditures. By 1986, oil prices were in "free fall." The price of crude oil, which had been $35 per barrel in late 1980 and early 1981, dropped to $10 per barrel in 1986, when cheating on output quotas spread throughout the cartel membership. OPEC member Saudi Arabia, the world's largest producer of crude, finally managed to restore order when it threatened to double its output if other OPEC members did not begin adhering to quotas. By the end of the decade, crude prices were hovering around $20 per barrel, where they returned after a short-lived upward blip during the Persian Gulf War. By 1995, in terms of inflation-adjusted dollars, crude oil prices had fallen by more than two-thirds since 1980.

The perils faced by cartels are also illustrated by the diamond market, where DeBeers, the famous diamond company, has controlled as much as 80 percent of the world supply. Although DeBeers itself produces only about 35 percent of the world's diamond output, it controls the marketing of another 45 percent through an outfit called the Central Selling Organization, or CSO. The CSO cartel has long restricted the sale of rough-cut diamonds to keep their prices at levels that maximize the profits of its members. One measure of the diamond cartel's success is the fact that in 1980, the wholesale price of investment-grade D-flawless diamonds—considered the most reliable measure of market conditions in the industry—was about $55,000 per carat. The recession of 1981–1982 caused a decline in the demand for all goods, particularly long-lived assets such as diamonds. Because the recession also sharply cut inflation, individuals no longer sought inflation hedges, further reducing the demand for collectibles and so-called hard assets. Despite DeBeers' best efforts to reduce the amount of diamonds on the market, prices of the gems dropped sharply. Downward pressure on prices was intensified by Australia's huge new Ashton mine, which began full-scale production in 1986 and which may have added as much as 40 percent to world diamond production. By 1987, the price of D-flawless gems was languishing between $14,000 and $17,000 per carat. After adjusting for inflation, by 1995 D-flawless diamonds were worth only about one-quarter of what they were worth in 1980.

Having seen the troubles that other cartels have gotten themselves into, we are now in a position to ask what happened to the communists? The answer (much to the chagrin of Marx, no doubt) is competition. When the Soviet Union dissolved, the two largest sturgeon fisheries fell under the jurisdictions of different autonomous republics, each of which wants to own and operate its own lucrative caviar business. Kazakhstan claims the fishery in the town of Gur'yev, while Russia claims the fishery in Astrakhan. Moreover, a variety of individuals, including enterprising Caspian Sea fishermen from these republics, are staking private claims, and in some cases trying to set up their own export channels (behavior officially termed "black market piracy"). The effect of this burgeoning capitalist behavior was a 20 percent drop in the official caviar export price during the first year of autonomy, plus an escalation of competition since then.

Caviar consumers are pleased at this turn of events, hoping that one day they may even be able to afford bargain beluga in Romanov-size portions. Old-line suppliers are not quite so happy. "We don't need this kind of competition," complains Sergei Dolya, who works for Sovrybflot, which used to control all Soviet caviar exports. "All of these small rivals mean that price will fall and the market will be ripped apart. This is a delicacy—we need to keep it elite." And so, just as Soviet citizens found that communism wasn't all that it was cracked up to be, it appears some of them are now learning that capitalism may be more than they bargained for—but perhaps no less than Karl Marx warned them about.

DISCUSSION QUESTIONS

1. Why are all cartels inherently unstable?

2. Would it be easier to form a cartel in a market with many producers or one with very few producers?

3. What will happen to the producers of caviar that is made from other types of fish eggs (such as salmon, whitefish, and trout) if the price of the finest sturgeon caviar continues to fall? Would these firms ever have an incentive to help the governments of Russia and Kazakhstan reestablish the caviar cartel?

4. If the members of your class were to attempt to form a study-reduction cartel in which everyone agreed to study less, which individuals would have the greatest to gain from the cartel? Which ones would have the most incentive to cheat on the cartel?

11

Faulty Prices

When the terms **monopoly** or **monopsony** are used, people usually think of giant industrial or commercial ventures that use market power to force prices into line with their preferences, much to the detriment of their customers or suppliers. At the beginning of the twentieth century, the Standard Oil Company (founded by John D. Rockefeller) was by far the largest petroleum firm in the nation. In many areas of the country it was the only seller of petroleum products, and used that monopoly advantage to extract prices above the competitive level. At about the same time in our history, many communities throughout the Allegheny and Appalachian mountain regions relied almost exclusively on coal mining for economic support. Typically, all mining operations in a given area were controlled by a single firm, which for all practical purposes was the single buyer of labor services in these communities. In this role as a monopsony, this single firm was able to force wage rates below the competitive level, for workers had no realistic alternative but to "take it or leave it" when the coal company announced what it was willing to pay.

Over the years, economists have come to use the terms monopoly and monopsony somewhat more broadly than implied by the literal translations of these words. Indeed, most commonly these words are now used simply to indicate that the firms involved have some influence over the prices at which they buy or sell goods, rather than having to take prices as completely given. There is also a growing awareness that governments, as well as businesses, can be thought of as being monopolies or monopsonies. For example, when the federal government, or even a state government, determines the taxes it will levy on its citizens, it can usefully be thought of as a monopoly provider of government services. Although higher taxes (the "price" of a government's product) may induce some citizens to depart for greener pastures (or lower taxes) elsewhere, governments have some discretion over the level of taxes. Thus, if a state increases its taxes by 10 percent relative to the taxes of a neighboring state, even though some individuals and businesses may choose to move elsewhere, not all of them will do so.

The monopoly power of governments extends beyond direct taxation of their own citizens. For example, the federal government can establish **tariffs** and **quotas** for imported goods, which reduce the amount of foreign-produced goods that may be sold in the United States. By reducing the supply of imported goods, quotas and tariffs raise the prices of those goods, benefiting domestic producers of those goods at the expense of U.S. consumers. In general, state governments in the United States are prohibited by the Constitution from imposing quotas or tariffs, either on goods from abroad or on goods coming in from other states.[1] The rationale for this prohibition is that states would otherwise try to protect their instate producers of goods from the competition of producers in other states. This would reduce the amount of mutually beneficial exchange among the citizens of the various states, yielding a loss in well-being for the citizenry as a whole.

Despite the constitutional prohibitions against state-imposed restrictions on interstate commerce, state governments do have a variety of powers under which they can regulate business within their state borders. Sometimes states use these powers to control activities that have important noneconomic features, as is the case with abortions and the sale of alcoholic beverages. In other cases, however, states are clearly attempting to use their monopoly or monopsony power to alter the prices of goods and services purchased by their citizens. Developments in the market for automobile insurance provide an excellent illustration of this behavior.

Those readers who are also drivers are no doubt aware that automobile insurance is expensive and getting more so every year. In some parts of the country, the cost of auto insurance has gone up 50 percent or more in inflation-adjusted dollars over the past decade. In states from California to New Jersey, proponents of insurance

---

[1] States have the power to impose taxes on goods, but they generally may not impose taxes on goods from other states higher than those they impose on goods produced in their own state.

"reform" have argued that the cause of the high and rising automobile insurance rates is monopoly behavior on the part of insurance companies. Thus state governments have begun to force insurance companies to rescind past rate increases and limit future increases. This movement began in California, where voters passed an initiative called Proposition 103. This measure required that auto insurance premiums be reduced by 20 percent and then frozen for a year. Then insurers were to be required to offer "good driver" rates that were 20 percent lower than any other rates—where the definition of a "good driver" included someone who had not been convicted of drunk driving within the past three years. Although Proposition 103 quickly became tied up in legal challenges, consumer groups in Florida started a petition to place an insurance rate reduction on their ballot, and groups in Pennsylvania began efforts to provide consumers with rate relief for their insurance rates. Soon thereafter, New Jersey passed legislation similar to California's Proposition 103.

In each case, these insurance "reforms" have been based on the argument that the insurance companies have been acting like monopolists, hiking rates above the competitive level. In fact, however, there are thousands of insurance companies across the country that sell automobile insurance. At any point in time, dozens (or even hundreds) of them are operating in any given state, competing with one another for business. If, somehow, the rates charged by any given firm were to rise above competitive levels, numerous other companies would be free to take away that company's business by offering lower rates. In short, the automobile insurance industry is highly competitive, and the high and rising rates across the country have nothing to do with "monopoly power" on the part of the firms selling insurance. Indeed, it is actually the *states* involved that are exerting market power.

Roughly one out of seven U.S. drivers resides in California. Pennsylvania, New Jersey, and Florida together account for almost another one-seventh of the nation's drivers. When a state represents a large proportion of the market for a good, its government can act on behalf of its citizens much like a monopsonist, forcing down the prices of the goods and services that firms sell within that state. This, in essence, is what is being done under the guise of auto insurance "reform." The state governments involved are trying to force down the price of the auto insurance purchased by their residents, just as monopsonist coal companies used to force down the wages of the labor services they purchased.

For suppliers, the legally mandated reduction in insurance premiums relative to their costs leads to a reduction in profits—and in a competitive industry, lower profits amount to losses. During the first full year of operation of Proposition 103, insurers in California reported $630 million in losses on their automobile insurance business. This raises the prospect that small intrastate insurers are likely to go out of business, while larger, interstate firms are likely to consider pulling out of the automobile insurance business in the affected states. Indeed, Allstate, the largest automobile insurance company in the state of New Jersey, announced that it was going to stop writing automobile insurance policies in the state. This reduction in the amount of insurance that firms are willing to supply has an uneven effect on drivers. Those who are lucky enough to get policies at the lower rates are clearly better off. But for many drivers, the impact of insurance reforms such as this will mean no auto insurance at all. Overall, the reduction in insurance coverage, relative to the free market amount, clearly produces a net loss in economic welfare.

Once we realize that the high cost of automobile insurance has nothing to do with monopoly on the part of insurers, we must ask what the cause of the high premiums might be. There are many forces at work, including rapidly escalating automobile repair costs, as well as rising costs of medical care for persons injured in accidents. Yet the basic structure of automobile insurance laws in most states—which requires that there be a finding of fault when there is an accident—is clearly one of the most important reasons that automobile insurance costs are so high. This is because automobile accidents quickly turn into lawsuits, particularly when someone is injured. As a result, when there is an automobile accident, not only must repair bills and doctor bills be paid, but lawyers' bills must be paid also—and the insurance premiums, on average, must include an allowance for all of the legal costs associated with accidents. In California, most automobile-injury cases are settled for less than $8000, and yet 60 percent of the cases end up involving litigation. Roughly one-third of the litigated settlement amounts go to lawyers as contingency fees-which means higher insurance rates for drivers.

Only three states—Florida, New York, and Michigan—have strict "no-fault" insurance laws. Under these laws, the costs of bodily injury from an accident, up to, say, $15,000 per injured person, are paid by the driver's own insurer, without any legal finding of responsibility. There are no lawsuits for such cases, and thus legal fees are drastically reduced. New York's no-fault law reduced automobile accident cases in the courts by 80 percent, and the state's automobile insurance premiums rose far more slowly than the national average as a result. Average automobile liability premiums in no-fault New York are 40 percent below rates in neighboring New Jersey, and it has been estimated that switching to strict no-fault offers motorists savings of $200 each in their annual premiums.

Although no-fault automobile insurance enables drivers to save substantially on automobile insurance premiums, don't hold your breath waiting for your state to switch to no-fault. The reason? Well, the big savings from no-fault insurance arise because lawyers are largely removed from the process. Switching to no-fault insurance requires that your state legislature change the automobile insurance laws, and most state legislators are—you guessed it—lawyers.

DISCUSSION QUESTIONS

1. What is the relationship between the type of automobile insurance reform discussed in this chapter and the rent controls discussed in Chapter 8?

2. When automobile insurance companies can no longer charge motorists the competitive price for insurance, are the companies likely to switch to other factors—such as race or age—to determine who will get insurance and who will not? Who is likely to gain and who to lose as a result?

3. Does a switch to no-fault insurance change the incentives of drivers? Will they be less careful when they are driving, knowing that if there is an accident the other driver's insurance will cover that person's bills?

4. Do you think that a state legislator would really vote against no-fault insurance just because he or she is a lawyer? Would you vote for legislation that reduced the demand for your services?

12

Inner City High Finance

Take a ride through virtually any low-income community and you will see billboards and other large signs advertising "check-cashing" services. At the beginning of the 1990s there were fewer than 2000 check cashers nationwide. Today, there are well over 5000 and the number is growing at a 10 percent annual rate. Along this same ride, you are also likely to see numerous pawn shops, offering "Quick Loans" or "Instant Cash." For many years in America, the number of pawnshops had been declining; but between 1986 and 1995, their yellow-page listings across the country more than doubled, to roughly 9500.

Is the spread of check-cashing services and the rebounding vitality of pawnshops related? And if so, why is their spread confined to inner-city areas, rather than across middle America or even into posh areas such as Beverly Hills or Palm Beach? The explanation for this rapid and peculiar change in the structure of inner-city financial markets can be found by examining some unintended consequences of regulation—specifically, consequences arising from Congress's expressed desire to rehabilitate the inner cities of America.

Our story begins roughly 20 years ago. During the 1970s, many members of Congress became concerned that the banking system was taking advantage of low-income, inner-city residents. Specifically, it was argued, although banks were happy to accept deposits from people and businesses located in inner-city areas, they were not interested in making loans to those very same people and firms. Because many of these inner-city residents and business owners were minorities, this behavior by banks was seen as discriminatory. Just as important, it was argued, is that the financial capital created in low-income neighborhoods wasn't getting recycled there; as a result, inner-city economic development was being stifled.

In an avowed effort to stimulate inner-city loans by banks, Congress passed the Community Reinvestment Act (CRA) of 1977. Under the terms of this act, banks were directed to make extra efforts to solicit loans in older and lower income neighborhoods, so that residents of these areas would be able to participate in, and indeed stimulate, the economic redevelopment of these inner-city areas.

Initially, the CRA had only a relatively modest impact. Over the last 10 years however, Congress and the key regulatory agencies charged with enforcing the act (the Comptroller of the Currency and the Federal Reserve) have intensified their efforts to strengthen the CRA, presumably in the hope of stimulating inner-city lending. Yet the result of these changes has been to substantially increase the regulatory burdens of the CRA, and to actually discourage banks from doing any business in the nation's inner cities.

For example, regulatory agencies have proposed that banks be required to produce data on the race, sex, and marital status of the owners of all businesses that request loans. In a slightly different vein, banks once received "credit" under the CRA for any of a variety of investments they made in small businesses; under more recent guidelines, banks are credited only if the investments benefit "low-and moderate-income geographies and persons." Even more important, however, is that when banks seek to expand their operations (e.g., by opening a branch) the regulatory agencies have begun scrutinizing in great detail whether or not existing branches of the bank are fulfilling their obligations under the CRA.

Presumably the new information on loan applicants is to be used by regulators to make sure the individual bank branches are making their quotas of loans to minority groups. Similarly, the new investment guidelines are intended to more carefully guide bank decisions so that quite specific individuals and businesses benefit from the CRA. And of course, by tying expansion approval to performance under the CRA, the intention is presumably to put additional teeth into the law's enforcement. In fact, the actual consequence of these and other features of the CRA has been to discourage banks from locating branches in low-income areas, and to close any existing branches in such areas.

Under the terms of the CRA, if a branch's deposits come from a particular low income area, then a certain minimum percentage of its loans and investments must go back into that area—virtually without regard to the profitability or risk associated with those loans and investments. Hence, any bank that has a branch in an inner-city area runs the risk of having its loan and investment decisions being made by a federal regulator on political grounds, rather than being made by its loan and investment officers on the basis of financial prudence. If federal regulators are unsatisfied with a bank's CRA performance, they can subject the bank to stiff penalties; just as important is the regulators' ability to prevent banks from expanding their operations into a new market area if they are dissatisfied with the bank's performance in an existing area.

Because the law ties loan requirements to areas where banks have deposits, the only sure way to avoid sanctions for not lending enough in the inner cities is to ensure that no deposits are coming from inner-city areas. Thus, if a bank has a branch in a low-income area, it has an incentive to close it; and if it was thinking of opening one there, those plans will almost surely be shelved. Although the CRA was intended to promote lending in low-income areas, its effect has been to discourage banks from locating there; on balance, it appears that the net effect of the legislation soon will be—or perhaps even now is—to actually *reduce* rather than increase lending in America's inner cities.

One of many examples of the law's impact on branch-banking decisions can be found in a comparison of the inner-city area known as South Central Los Angeles with the more affluent city of Gardena, located right next door. Because of a massive exodus of banks over the last 10 years, there are only 20 bank branches serving the 260,000 residents of South Central L.A., but 133 fee-charging, check-cashing outlets. In neighboring Gardenia, which has a population of only 50,000, there are only a handful of check-cashing services, but there are 21 bank branches. Across the country in the New York City area, 14 percent of Brooklyn's bank branches closed between 1980 and 1994; most of those closures came in the lower-income areas of the borough. And in low-income Bedford-Stuyvesant, there are only 3 bank branches to serve 129,000 people.

Into the void come check-cashing services. Most outlets charge 1.5 percent to 6 percent of the face value of the check to cash it, but their fees can run as high as 10 percent for an out-of-state or other risky check. Once customers receive their money, many of them then buy money orders—at 50 cents to $1 apiece—to pay their bills. Overall, check-cashing patrons can easily pay more than triple the fees they would pay for low-cost checking accounts at banks. One New York study, for example, found that the typical annual "banking" services consumed by a person bringing home $650 every two weeks would cost $232 if performed by a check-cashing service, but only $68 if done by a bank. Of course the check casher is in the neighborhood, while the nearest bank may be a thirty-minute bus ride away, so the apparent economy of the bank is no economy at all. For those people who find it inconvenient to leave their homes or job sites there is even an outfit offering "Mobile Money" check-cashing trucks that will come to the customer's location to "turn paper into cash" for a fee.

Some check-cashing outlets have also gone into the lending business—although they typically don't call it this. They make the loans by taking "post-dated" checks from customers. Customers pay a fee to get cash immediately, along with an agreement that their checks will not be cashed until their next payday. For example, a customer might write a check for $300, receiving in return $250 in immediate cash, together with an agreement that the check will be held until the next payday. The $50 fee represents 20 percent of the money loaned. On an annualized basis, if the check is held for two weeks, that represents an interest rate of over 500 percent!

The departure of banks from inner cities has also stimulated borrowing from pawn shops, which are lending institutions where a person can borrow money on items that are pawned—that is, left with the pawnshop as security for the loan. The customer is given a pawn ticket and a certain amount of cash, say, 50 percent of the wholesale value of the pawned item. Every month, the pawnshop charges a "fee" for keeping the pawned item, so that the amount that must be repaid to reclaim the item increases over time. These monthly fees can amount to the equivalent of annual rates of interest between 100 and 300 percent.

The market void created by the Community Reinvestment Act has turned inner-city high finance into big business. Indeed, there are now even publicly traded chains of pawn shops springing up throughout the country. Cash America, started by Jack Daugherty, has over 230 outlets, generating about $150 million in revenues and $15 million in net income. The value of the shares of stock in Cash

America has increased dramatically in the decade that the stock has been on the market.

If the decline in bank branches continues, there are likely to be many more Jack Daughertys and Mobile Money trucks providing services in the future. As the deputy superintendent of banks in New York puts it, such institutions "serve a purpose in the real world." And what of the high fees and service charges that customers pay for the services of check cashers and pawnshops? Rick Price, whose family runs six check-cashing stores in the New York metropolitan area, notes that "We're no different than people out there selling sneakers to kids in poor neighborhoods. . . . Our prices are an economic hardship only if they are compared against 'free.'"

DISCUSSION QUESTIONS

1. What would be the likely consequences if the fees of check cashers and pawn shops were controlled by law?

2. How would one determine if the fees charged by check cashers and pawn shops were "too high"? What would we observe if they were high relative to the costs of the services they provide?

3. Other federal regulations prohibit banks from making loans that the bank regulators consider to be "too risky." How have these regulations likely influenced banks' decisions to leave low-income inner-city areas?

4. Is it possible that the CRA could actually lead to *less* lending in inner-city areas than would be observed without the law? Explain why or why not.

13

Getting Scalped

Kevin Thomas didn't even finish high school in the Bronx. Nevertheless, he works seven nights a week and earns about $40,000 a year. By the time he turned 26, he had $75,000 in savings. To many people in New York City, Kevin Thomas provides the same service that any other retailer provides—he sells something they want at a price they are willing to pay. For others, however, including various New York State and City law-enforcement authorities, Mr. Thomas is a criminal. No, Kevin Thomas doesn't deal in drugs; he is a ticket broker.

Anyone who has ever tried to get a ticket to a popular rock concert or sports event knows that using "normal" ticket channels may be unproductive. Often, by the time you decide you want to purchase your tickets, the local official ticket agencies are sold out. Enter the ticket scalper. This colorful term is used because normally when you purchase a ticket that is being resold, you pay a higher price—you get "scalped."

For example, the scalpers' prices for tickets to the Rolling Stones' 1994 "Voodoo Lounge" concert tour routinely ranged from twice the face value up to five times face value for prime seats. Tickets to the 1993 baseball All-Star game sold on the street for $1000 despite their stated value of $60. And in 1995 the best tickets to the Super Bowl went for up to $1200 each.

Twenty-six states, plus most cities with professional sports franchises, have laws on the books that make it illegal to resell tickets at a price that exceeds the face amount by more than a small amount. In some states, such as South Carolina, the resale price cannot exceed the face amount by more than a fixed dollar

86

amount, say $1. In New York it is illegal to resell tickets for more than $5 or 10 percent above their face value, whichever is greater. Consequently, in 1994, New York Attorney General G. Oliver Coppell brought suit against two New Jersey ticket brokers who "scalped" tickets to a Barbra Streisand concert. In his complaint, the Attorney General claimed that the brokers charged up to $350 each for tickets "worth" only $125 each. Of course, that statement is patently false: if the tickets were not worth $350 to the purchasers, they would not have voluntarily bought them. The tickets may have had a face value of $125, but their worth in the marketplace was clearly greater. At $125, the quantity demanded was greater than the quantity supplied. The ticket scalpers took advantage of this disequilibrium to make a **profit,** for they ended up selling the tickets at a price closer to the **market clearing price**—$350 each.

We must begin by asking the most basic question about ticket scalping: Why are the services of scalpers needed in the first place? Clearly, those who set official ticket prices for Broadway musicals, rock concerts, and sports events sometimes do not set market clearing prices. When the organizers of a Broadway musical, for example, charge the same price for a ticket on Saturday night as they do on Tuesday night, they are almost guaranteed that the quantity demanded will exceed the quantity supplied by a greater amount on Saturday night than on Tuesday night—provided the musical is a hit. When rock promoters set the same price for the best seats as they do for the remaining seats, they are almost guaranteed that the quantity of the best seats demanded at that price will exceed the quantity supplied.

Sometimes the demand for scalpers' services arises simply due to a mistake in pricing. There is always some uncertainty regarding just how popular a sporting or other entertainment event is going to be. Given this uncertainty, even if promoters usually judge the market correctly, there will be times when they err. When they overestimate the demand for the product, there will be tickets left over; in this case, and when the promoters have judged demand exactly, no one will be interested in the services of a scalper. But in those cases when the demand for the product has been underestimated, the resulting excess demand for the product must be rationed somehow—which is where the scalpers come in.

It is evident, however, that mistakes cannot account for all of the scalping that is observed. The All Star game, the Super Bowl, and the NCAA Final Four in basketball sell out *every* year, typically by huge margins. For example, there were 553,000 applications for the 1993 Final Four, held in Charlotte, North Carolina, although the Charlotte Coliseum has only about 20,000 seats. Similarly, sellouts for the 1996 Olympics in Atlanta were so well anticipated that a law prohibiting scalping was passed two years before the Olympics took place! Thus, we may safely conclude that many sellouts are no surprise, and yet they continue to occur and continue to provide a market niche for scalpers.

Why such permanent conditions of apparent disequilibrium persist is not fully understood by economists. But Professor Gary Becker, winner of the Nobel Prize in economics, has proposed one explanation that has attracted some supporters.[1] He argues that individual demands for some goods depend on the demands by other consumers. This may be true, for example, because the consumption of things such as concerts and sporting events is importantly a social event, made more enjoyable by being consumed in the company of other people. Certainly anyone who has been to a major rock concert or football game can attest to the excitement that flows through a jam-packed crowd.

According to Becker's explanation, it is absolutely crucial to the promoters of such events that they be "sellouts." If consumers do not believe that they must actively compete with one another for tickets that are not available for everyone at the stated price, they will quickly lose interest in the event. This in turn will cause a large decrease in demand and a sharp drop in the promotor's profits. Thus, promoters price the tickets low enough to ensure a sellout, and the scalpers are left to "fine-tune" the price at which the sellout will occur.

In discussions of ticket scalping, two issues often seem to arise. The first of these involves the concept of fairness. Is it "fair" that those who are willing to pay more are able to purchase black-market tickets from ticket scalpers? What about those people who cannot "afford" to pay such high prices, even if they want those tickets badly? Economists have little to say about the concept of fairness, for it is a normative concept, that is, a concept that in-

---

[1] Gary Becker, "A Note on Restaurant Pricing and Other Examples of Social Influences on Prices," *Journal of Political Economy,* Vol. 99, no. 5, 1991, pp. 1109–16.

volves inherently personal value judgements that may differ from person to person.

We can point out, however, that the same argument can be used with respect to virtually any highly prized goods or services, such as luxury cars, prime beef, high-quality restaurant meals, Picasso paintings, ski vacations, and the latest and fastest home computers. All that economists can say is that if price is used to allocate a scarce good or service, then resources are allocated efficiently.

By definition, every time there is a sellout to any event, ticket prices are below the market clearing level. Sellouts indicate that there must be some individuals who place a greater value on the entertainment event than the actual face money price of such tickets. In the absence of scalpers, those individuals would not attend the event, implying that the value received by consumers would not be at its highest level. Thus, scalpers ensure that the effective highest-valued use is made of the tickets.

The second issue that routinely arises is how scalpers are able to come up with seemingly huge numbers of tickets despite the inability of consumers to get as many tickets as they want at box-office prices. Actually, there is very little mystery around the success of the scalpers in getting tickets. Some tickets are purchased legally, directly from the theater or stadium operators. Some scalpers hire people to stand in line to purchase tickets on their behalf, a practice that is also generally legal. But not all of the practices are above board. Indeed, it is generally acknowledged that box-office personnel often work with scalpers, illicitly setting aside blocks of the best tickets for a kickback, known as "ice."

Whatever the method used in a particular situation, the brokers face a gamut of obstacles in their path, not all of them easy to understand. For example, although scalping is illegal in New York, neighboring New Jersey does not restrict ticket prices. Thus it is legal for New Jersey scalpers to sell higher-priced tickets to readers of New Jersey newspapers, but not to those who read newspapers whose main office is in New York. If this seems strange to you, it also seems strange to Kevin Thomas, the New York ticket broker. As he remarked, "I look at scalping like working as a stockbroker, buying low and selling high. If people are willing to pay me the money, what kind of problem is that?"

DISCUSSION QUESTIONS

1. If Becker's explanation of underpricing is correct, would promoters of concerts and sporting events favor or oppose a law that made scalping illegal?

2. It is typically the best seats that are underpriced the most. For example, at a rock concert, all tickets usually have the same box-office price even though there are clear differences in the quality of the seats, and thus many more people want the better seats at the uniform price. Can you suggest an explanation for this observation?

3. It is typically the best games that are underpriced the most. For example, playoff games are much more likely to be underpriced more than are regular season games. Can you suggest an explanation for this observation?

4. What do your answers to the previous questions imply about how first class seats on airplanes should be priced relative to economy-class seats on those planes?

Part Four

Factor Markets

INTRODUCTION

In one sense, factors of production—such as land, labor and capital—are no different from other economic goods. After all, they are scarce goods and thus the basic tools used by economists can be applied to understand the markets for them. Nevertheless, particularly when the factor of production is labor, special care is sometimes required. For a variety of reasons, not everything is what it seems to be on the surface.

Perhaps the first consideration that comes to the mind of a factor owner is the economic return that she or he can earn. In Chapter 14, "The Economic Returns to Education," we examine the rate of return to getting a college education. Recent evidence indicates that this return is high (by historical standards) and recently has been rising. We explore the reasons behind these findings and—perhaps more importantly for readers of this book—consider what is likely to happen to the returns to a college education in the future.

One determinant of the earnings of any factor of production is the supply of that factor. In the case of labor, one of the key forces that influence supply is immigration, both legal and illegal. After several decades of decline, immigration into the United States has been rising in recent years. Indeed, it is now at its highest levels in more than seventy years. Why this has happened and what effects it will have are the focus of Chapter 15, "Tired, Poor, Huddled Masses." For the economy as a whole, immigration almost certainly yields positive net benefits. Yet immigration potentially also has important effects on the distribution of wealth among individuals. For this reason, and because the benefits produced by immigration are affected by the identity of the immigrants, economic analysis can shed important insights on the costs and benefits of alternative immigration policies.

Immigration is not the only force that is changing today's labor markets. As we see in Chapter 16, "Disposable Workers," the entry of women into the labor force and the growth of international competition have helped change the nature of many jobs. Growing numbers of people have become disposable workers, thereby earning lower wages, receiving fewer fringe benefits, and enjoying little job security. Much of the concern over the growth of the disposable workforce has focused on its potential costs, including reduced worker loyalty and possibly lower levels of training. Yet the contingent job relationships inherent in this type of employment also yield benefits to both employers and workers themselves. Most things in life produce both benefits and costs, and the disposable worker is no exception.

If part-time and temporary workers are at one end of the labor market spectrum, highly-paid professional athletes are surely at the other—even though their average job tenure may be no greater. In Chapter 17, "Million Dollar Men," we examine the seemingly peculiar market for professional athletes. In recent years, salaries for these factors of production have soared—yet the athletes go on strike demanding even more. The market prices of professional sports franchises have risen almost as fast as the salaries of the players—and yet the owners complain that they are losing money. Is this market for labor services fundamentally different from any other labor market? As we shall see, economic analysis can once again provide us with some surprising insights.

Our final foray into the labor market asks what is likely to happen when the government interferes with its operation. Thus, in Chapter 18, we examine "The Effects of the Minimum Wage." As we shall see time and again in this book, the effects of government actions are not always what they seem, nor are they usually what their proponents claim for them. The chief losers from the minimum wage are often the very people who can least afford those losses, while those who claim to support the law on altruistic grounds are in fact likely to be the biggest winners. The message of this chapter may well be this simple piece of advice: When someone claims to be doing something *for* you, it is time to ask what that person is doing *to* you.

14

The Economic Returns to Education

How much should you study? This is surely a question that must interest readers of this book. Not surprisingly, we'll find that economics can help you answer this question—and best of all, answer it in a way that will make you better off.

Every time you study one hour, you incur an **opportunity cost**—namely, the value of using that time in its next-best (next highest-valued) alternative. You might be making a choice between spending that hour studying for an economics exam versus studying for another exam. Alternatively, you might be choosing between studying one more hour and talking to your friends one more hour. In any event, there is always an alternative use of your time, and thus there is always a cost involved in studying.

You probably already know that businesses continue producing up to the point at which the **marginal revenue** or additional revenue from one more unit of output, is just equal to the additional cost of that unit. Applying such a rule to your decisions yields the following proposition regarding your study time: You will always want to study up to the point at which the marginal benefit of studying just equals the marginal cost, which in this case amounts to the opportunity cost—the highest-valued alternative use of your time.

The analysis that is useful in evaluating the number of hours you should study is applicable to other educational questions: How many years of education should you obtain? Is a college education really worth effort? If so, wouldn't an advanced degree be even better?

Questions such as these usually begin to be raised in earnest when people are in junior high school. Parents, relatives, and other adults begin emphasizing that education is important, indeed, often arguing that it is the most important activity a person will ever undertake. And at that point in a person's life, it is likely that such arguments are correct. By the time people are in high school they are told by the same well-meaning adults that college is a great thing—and it is for most people. But then sometimes it is claimed that young people should "get all the education they can get." That's when well-meaning advice turns into misleading nonsense.

If you were to literally get all the education possible, you would plan a higher-education career consisting of a bachelor's degree, a master's degree, one (or more!) Ph.D.s, and several post-doctoral fellowships. Then, indeed, you would be getting all the education you could get. Some people actually do that, but not very many. In fact, only a small percentage of adults go to graduate school and get an advanced degree. Despite what your parents may have told you, those people who do *not* get advanced degrees are more than likely behaving rationally.

What does "rational" mean in this instance? It means applying the basic principle we laid out at the beginning of this chapter. If the objective is to allocate time efficiently, one should not engage in any activity past the point at which the marginal benefit of that activity falls below its marginal cost. Going to school year after year eventually leads to the point at which marginal cost exceeds marginal benefit.

This occurs for two reasons. On the one hand, the incremental benefit of learning new skills eventually starts decreasing as you continue to increase the inputs—your time, work effort, and money. At the same time, the marginal cost of continuing your education is rising as your education takes place. Why is the marginal cost increasing? Because as you obtain more education and get older, your earning capacity goes up. That means that your opportunity cost of not working (your foregone income because you are still in school) goes up. Eventually, with declining marginal benefits and rising marginal costs, the benefits of an additional unit of education will drop below the added costs, implying that it is time to stop getting educated and time to start *using* your education.

Ultimately, the only way you can rationally determine whether getting a college degree is worthwhile is to know what the **rate of**

return to that education will be. Two economists, Orley Ashenfelter and Alan Krueger, have come up with some fairly convincing results that imply that staying in school pays off, at least over the range of schooling most relevant to you. They studied the returns to education earned by hundreds of identical twins. The twins were utilized so that the researchers could control for the possible influence of genetic factors. Moreover, given that all the twins faced essentially the same home environment, the researchers were able to control for those factors, too. Having controlled for these key factors (and a variety of other, less important forces) Ashenfelter and Krueger discovered that each additional year of schooling increased wages by roughly 13 to 16 percent. Overall, this means that for four years of college, an individual's expected annual income would go up to $36,000 from $21,600—an increase of 67 percent.

These estimates are considerably higher than those obtained by previous researchers. Are the new estimates plausible? Interestingly enough, data for 1993 showed that college graduates actually earned 75 percent more than otherwise comparable high school graduates. So the highly sophisticated methods used by Ashenfelter and Krueger are in general agreement with what simple numbers would suggest. Given these facts, it is perhaps not surprising that almost 65 percent of high school graduates in the United States are now enrolling in colleges. A little more than a decade ago, less than 55 percent were enrolling.

But these high college enrollment rates suggest a seeming puzzle. Supply and demand analysis predicts that if supply rises relative to demand, the relative price of the good (in this case, college graduates) should fall. In the current context, it *appears* that the supply of college graduates is rising relative to the demand for them. If this is true, why is the income premium so great for those who complete college?

To understand the current situation and to help predict the future, we must look back into the 1970s. At that time the supply of college graduates as a proportion of the total work force was growing at about 4.3 percent a year. During the 1980s, in contrast, this proportion grew at only about 2.5 percent a year. Not surprisingly, the premium that employers were willing to pay for college degree holders rose during the 1980s, actually doubling. So supply and demand were clearly at work then. The demand for college degree holders was growing faster than the supply of college degree holders, and thus the returns to higher education rose. Enter the 1990s. Although, as we just mentioned, the proportion of high school graduates going to college has increased, the number of American youths graduating from high school is falling. That is because the so-called baby-bust generation is upon us. A decade ago, high schools were graduating 3.1 million students a year; today they are only graduating 2.5 million a year. Thus, although a higher proportion is going on to college, a smaller total number is doing so. For the time being, the demand for college graduates seems to be rising at least as fast as the supply of those graduates. So, if you are reading this book as part of a college course, you are probably right where you ought to be, doing just what you should be doing. But don't delay your graduation too long: Demographers are predicting that total college enrollments are likely to begin rising around 1998. If the expected surge of new college-educated workers materializes around the year 2000, the students reading this book then may be considerably less pleased to hear what is happening at that time to the economic returns to education.

DISCUSSION QUESTIONS

1. Why do you think it is important to take into account (or control for) genetic and environmental factors when estimating the rate of return to education?

2. If the total number of students enrolled in college has been shrinking (relative to the population), what do you think has been happening to the salaries of your professors (relative to the salaries of other workers)? If demographers are correct about likely increases in college enrollments in the future, what will likely happen to faculty salaries as a result?

3. What role do you think that shrinking college enrollments might have played in the "grade inflation" that has taken place over the last 15 to 20 years? What impact will rising enrollments in the future likely have on grades?

4. With undergraduate college enrollments expected to rise in the not too distant future, what do you predict will happen to the returns to *graduate* education?

15

Tired, Poor, Huddled Masses

Despite the Statue of Liberty's justly famous welcome to America's newcomers, immigration remains a lightning rod for political and social controversy. Much of the debate focuses on illegal immigration: How should we prevent it, and how should we respond when people illegally succeed in breaching our shores? But much of the debate also has addressed whether _any_ immigration into the United States should be permitted, and if so, just who should be granted that right.

The issue of immigration has gained far more attention in recent years because of the upsurge in it since the 1960s. There are nearly 25 million foreign-born persons now in America—about 9 percent of the total population. Nevertheless, measured as a proportion of the population, immigrants are far less significant than they were in years past. Between 1880 and 1920, for example, foreign-born persons typically comprised 15 percent of the population. Subsequent legal restrictions reduced the influx of immigrants sharply, leading to a 40-year decline in the proportion of the U.S. population that was foreign-born. It has only been in the last 30 years that the foreign-born proportion has begun to rebound.

This rebound was itself caused by a change in federal immigration policy. In 1965, perhaps influenced by the mood of the civil rights movement, the United States started to do away with quotas that favored white Europeans. Instead, the federal government made family unification the centerpiece of immigration policy. As a result, children, spouses, and siblings poured in from around the world to join immigrants who had originally entered alone. This flood was further stimulated by growing sentiment that individuals fleeing communist persecution should receive special status as refugees. Additional entry visas were set aside for such refugees, thereby pushing immigration totals above what they would have been.

Most immigration—two-thirds or more—is legal, so we shall begin by looking at the effects of immigration in general. By definition, immigration entails an influx of individuals from other locations. The inflow stimulates both the supply of labor and the demand for goods and services. In labor markets, although the overall result will be a rise in total employment, the new arrivals may also tend to depress wage rates. This is said to be a particular concern regarding the markets for low-skill jobs, because of the lower average skills possessed by new immigrants. If immigration depresses wage rates in these markets, some native-born workers may become unemployed or drop out of the labor force altogether. Much of the adverse sentiment toward immigration has been stimulated by this potential negative impact on low-skilled American workers.

Superficially, at least, there appears to besome basis for this concern. Most new immigrants are clearly committed to making their way in the labor force: the Urban Institute estimates, for example, that about 74 percent of adult male immigrants hold jobs, versus 72 percent of the overall male population. A number of studies have examined whether this influx of immigrant workers has adversely affected native-born workers; all of the researchers have come to essentially the same conclusion—little or no negative impact on employment or unemployment rates of less-skilled natives.[1]

There are at least two possible reasons for the minimal adverse impact of immigrants on native workers. First, the demand for unskilled labor may be highly responsive to even small changes in wages. Under such circumstances, an increase in the supply of labor results chiefly in a rise in employment, rather than a wage decrease that would push native-born workers out of employment. Second, new immigrants seem to chiefly compete for low-skilled jobs with other immigrants, not with Americans. The garment industry of New York is a prime example: recent arrivals from Latin America, the Caribbean, and the Far East sit at machines once operated by Italians and Jews. On balance, then, the arrival of new immigrants

---

[1] See George Borjas, *Friends or Strangers: The Impact of Immigrants on the U.S. Economy*, (New York, Basic Books, 1990). Borjas's conclusions have been reinforced by more recent studies.

boosts employment overall. For example, in examining the 400 largest counties in the United States, one study found that for every 100-person increase in the population of adult immigrants, the number of new jobs rose by 46, while for every 100 new native-born Americans, the number of new jobs rose by just 25.

On the demand side of the market, many immigrants initially have relatively low incomes and thus are most likely to consume basic staple items, such as food, used cars, and inexpensive clothing. But—and this is a key source of contention in those areas of the country that have received the brunt of immigration—new immigrants are also likely to be consumers of publicly provided or subsidized services, such as public transportation, education, and some forms of health care. Indeed, the adverse impact that new immigration sometimes has on state and local budgets is often its most visible and easily quantifiable measure, and thus also an important source of opposition to immigration. At times, this opposition can reach extraordinary lengths. Thus, in California, voters passed Proposition 187, a 1994 ballot initiative that stripped illegal immigrants of rights to many expensive government services, including education and nonemergency health care.

With a million or so immigrants streaming into the United States each year, the potential fiscal burden on government, particularly at the state and local level, is considerable. As we shall see, there is merit to the concerns over the cost to taxpayers of new immigration. Yet this concern is also somewhat misplaced.

One measure of the potential adverse impact of immigration lies in the fact that although only 8.4 percent of households in America are foreign-born, they receive 13.1 percent of public assistance. In California, foreign households receive a whopping 32 percent of all public cash assistance. But these overall numbers mask the fact that the behavior of immigrants is far from uniform. Roughly two-thirds of all immigrants arrive legally under the regular immigration system. They generally are well-educated and highly motivated, and are little more likely than natives (7.8 percent versus 7.4 percent) to receive welfare payments. There seems little doubt that these individuals contribute positively to the fiscal well-being of government at all levels, paying more in taxes than they receive in government benefits.

The story is much different for the other one-third of all immigrants, comprised of illegal immigrants, as well as legal immigrants arriving as refugees from former Communist countries. The refugees in particular impose a significant drain on government coffers. Overall, receipt of welfare among refugees is 16 percent, double that of other legal immigrants; among recent refugee arrivals, 31 percent are on welfare. And although illegal immigrants typically may not receive any cash assistance, many are regular consumers of other forms of taxpayer-funded public assistance. One study estimated, for example, that during the early 1990s a majority of the births in the Los Angeles area were to illegal immigrant mothers, paid for chiefly with public funds.

The sharp difference in behavior between refugees and illegal immigrants on the one hand, and regular immigrants on the other hand, is probably due in part to the illegal immigrants' and refugees' lower educational levels (and thus lower earning capacity) than those of either regular-status immigrants or native-born individuals. But at least as important regarding the behavior of refugees are the sharp differences in government policy toward regular and refugee immigrants. For example, regular-status immigrants are not eligible for welfare until they have been in the country for at least three to five years. In contrast, refugees from countries such as Laos, Cambodia, Vietnam, the former Soviet Union, and Cuba are immediately eligible for welfare, as well as for a wide range of benefits exceeding even what native-born Americans get. Welfare receipt rates among these groups range from 16 percent among Cubans, up to 49 percent among Cambodians.

Whatever immigrant groups we are discussing, California is likely to figure prominently in the debate. This is hardly surprising, because more new immigrants live in California than in any other state. And on the illegal immigration front, California is even more of a national leader. Of the 4 million or so illegal immigrants who are estimated to reside in the United States, roughly 1.6 million of them—about 40 percent—are believed to live in the Golden State.

Given the prominence of California in the immigration debate, it is useful to ask why so many immigrants—particularly illegal immigrants—have been attracted there. Partly the answer is geography, for California not only shares a border with Mexico; it also has a vast shoreline and major ports that beckon potential arrivals from the Far East. Also important, however, is that the flood of immigrants to the Golden State, particularly illegal immigrants, has been the result of policies pushed for by Californians. For example, in

1984 and 1985, Los Angeles, San Francisco, and many other municipalities in California declared their cities to be sanctuaries for illegal
immigrants from Central American governments that were regarded as centers of political repression. Then, in 1986, the
California Congressional delegation held up passage of the
Immigration and Reform Act until a provision was added to allow
several hundred thousand immigrants into the country temporarily
so that they could help harvest crops, predominantly in agriculture-
rich California.

Under the so–called guest worker provisions that eventually resulted, about 1.1 million immigrants entered the United States and
won legal status. Most of them settled in California, attracted by
wages that were up to 10 times as high as those payable in their
countries of origin. These new legal immigrants proved a powerful
attraction for their families, who soon began arriving in large—and
chiefly illegal—numbers. The women and children who comprised
these families were the ones most likely to use the government services, such as education and health care, denied them under the provisions of Proposition 187. Thus, as the deputy chief of staff to the
California Governor notes, when it comes to illegal immigration, "in
some ways there have been self-inflicted wounds."

DISCUSSION QUESTIONS

1. Why are the opponents of immigration likely to be more vocal
   than are the supporters of immigration?

2. How do the costs of immigration change relative to the benefits
   as the value of publicly provided or subsidized services rise in
   real terms?

3. What would happen to the composition of immigrants if, as suggested by Nobel Prize–winning economist Gary Becker, the
   United States began auctioning off entry visas to potential immigrants who were willing and able to pay the most money for
   the right to enter the country legally?

4. If one perceived communist countries to be a threat to the U.S.,
   would it make good economic sense to offer special refugee status to persons emigrating from communist nations?

16

Disposable Workers

Pete Reformat survived economic upheaval by becoming a disposable worker. He was a pipe fitter for USX Corporation in its Gary, Indiana, plant, making $13 per hour and entitled to a full range of fringe benefits, such as health insurance. Then he was laid off—and immediately rehired by a USX subcontractor who put him to work in the same USX plant. Pete was not entirely happy with this arrangement. His base pay dropped to $5 per hour, he lost his fringe benefits, and job security went out the window. But at least he had a job.

Confronted with a rapidly changing labor force and growing international competition, USX Corporation is one of thousands of American companies now using contingent workers. Often just as skilled as "permanent" workers next to them on the job, contingent workers—also referred to as **disposable workers**—typically earn lower wages, receive fewer fringe benefits, and enjoy little job security. It is not surprising that many corporations have found them to be attractive employees. As a result, the number of disposable workers rose sharply between 1980 and 1985, and by the mid-1990s, even middle- and upper-level *executives* had joined their ranks, thus becoming "disposable bosses." Indeed, if all part-time employees are counted as part of the disposable group, contingent workers now total about 30 percent of the entire labor force.

Of the 35,000,000 or more contingent workers in the economy, roughly half are part-time employees, putting in up to 32 hours a week on the job. Among full-timers, many work at home, doing tasks that range from knitting ski caps to programming computers. Also, at any point in time, more than 1.5 million work as "temporaries," placed by agencies such as Kelly Services and Manpower Temporary Services. But the group of full-time contingent workers that has grown the fastest is comprised of persons who are employed by subcontractors of firms that ultimately enjoy their services, and those who are simply "leased."

Subcontracting is nothing new, of course. The construction industry has long used this practice. Basically, a prime contractor oversees and guarantees the finished product, but relies on independent subcontractors ("subs") to actually perform the various tasks—carpentry, plumbing, or wiring—involved in producing the final product. What is new is that the practice of subcontracting has spread to an incredible diversity of industries—automobiles, steel fabricating, electronics, and even high-tech computer firms. Indeed, it has been estimated that work done by subs now accounts for 70 percent of the value of each car that the Chrysler Corporation makes. Nationwide, employees of subcontractors have more than doubled in number since 1980.

Even more than subcontracting, employee leasing appears to be a child of the last decade. The leasing process begins with a firm that "fires" its workers, who are immediately "hired" by an outside firm. The sole function of the outside firm is to process the workers' paychecks and administer their fringe benefits—using money provided by the original employer. Employee leasing enables the outside firms to "pool" workers from a variety of different companies; hence they can bargain for cheaper group rates on fringe benefits such as health insurance. It also allows professionals such as doctors and lawyers to get around federal legislation requiring small business employees to be covered by the same pension and medical plans as the owners. Finally, because the original firms are committed to the leased employees for only as long as it suits them, employee leasing enables firms to shift some of the risk of business fluctuations to workers. Given these advantages, it is little wonder that by 1995 firms were leasing over a million workers—despite the fact that the arrangement was effectively unknown 15 years before.

How are we to account for the remarkable growth in disposable jobs? First, and probably most important, there is the dramatic change in the composition of the work force. Prior to the 1960s, the majority of jobs were held by adult males. Beginning late in that decade, however, the postwar baby-boom generation began to stream into the work force. During the 1970s, that stream became a torrent and was intensified by the entry of unprecedented numbers of women looking for jobs. And although the baby–boom bulge began to recede in the 1980s, the entry of women to the labor force continued apace. Between 1965 and 1985, the labor force grew by 41 million persons. Fully 23 percent of these new workers were under age 25, and 61 percent were women. Over the same period of time, the **labor force participation rate** of women grew from 39 percent to more than 54 percent; by 1995, some 60 percent of all women were participating in the labor force.

The impact of these changes has been profound. Many younger workers, aged 16 to 24, simply don't know what career they want. For them, a short-term job—perhaps for a summer or even as long as a year—is a way of finding out what they like and don't like to do. Or they may want to finish their education and thus are unwilling to commit to more than a summer job, unless it can be part-time and offer flexible hours during the school year. Moreover, young people tend to have less experience and fewer skills than their elders; if the only jobs available were high-paying, few employers would hire youths—leaving them without the experience and skills needed to get high-paying jobs. Finally, many young workers are covered by their parents' fringe-benefit programs. And even if they are not, it is clear that health and life insurance (or pensions!) are less important to an unmarried 20-year-old than to a 40-year-old head of household with a spouse and children. All in all, the relatively lower pay, fewer benefits, and flexible jobs *exactly* fit the bill for younger workers.

For the women who have entered the workforce in record numbers, the picture is slightly different. Many women have committed themselves to a career in the workplace rather than in the home and have the educational background to help them succeed. For them, disposable jobs are of little interest, particularly if they are single and seeking job security and a full package of fringe benefits. Other women have been "pushed" into the work force, perhaps owing to divorce or the death of a spouse. For them, contingent employment, even if it is just part-time, may be the only alternative to welfare. Yet there are also many women for whom flexible jobs with few fringe benefits are the ideal solution. In many cases, women are covered by the benefit programs of their spouses. These women may find that jobs with good fringe benefits necessitate giving up too much take-home pay in return for redundant insurance or pension coverage. And if there are small children at home, working part-time or at home allows women to supplement their spouse's income without disrupting family life. In short, the substantial increase of working women has, on average, increased the appeal of contingent employment.

The second reason for the popularity of disposable employees lies in the flexibility they permit over the business cycle. During the stable and prosperous 1950s and 1960s, businesses had developed long-term contracts to assure themselves of loyal, dedicated employees who would be around year after year. Major recessions in 1973–74, 1980–82, and 1990–91 led to layoffs even among senior workers—who traditionally had felt their jobs were virtually guaranteed. The result was widespread resentment and a plunge in worker morale and thus productivity. Even the number of lawsuits brought by workers for "wrongful dismissal"—on the grounds that they had been assured continued employment—rose sharply. Firms began to rethink their employment strategies, and the use of contingent workers was one of the solutions that evolved. As one manager of Apple Computer, Inc., put it, "If we bring someone on board full-time, there is an implied obligation that the job won't disappear. But that can happen in an industry as volatile as ours." Seeking to escape some of this risk, many firms found members of the rapidly changing labor force willing to absorb it.

The opportunity to hire part-time or temporary workers rather than permanent, full-time employees can generate higher employment than would otherwise be the case. During the early stages of economic recovery from recession, firms are understandably reluctant to form permanent attachments with new employees. Rather than simply have existing workers put in more overtime, some firms hire disposable workers. If the recovery turns out to be sustained, many of the temporary and part-time hires will end up getting permanent, full-time jobs. And if the recovery fizzles, at least those persons will have had some work rather than none. Either way, unemployment is reduced.

The final element in the disposable worker story has to do with the rise in international competition over the last twenty years. Between 1975 and 1995, American imports grew sharply relative to the rest of the economy, rising to nearly 10 percent of the value of the nation's total annual output, or **gross domestic product (GDP).** Much of this new import penetration came from countries in the Far East and South America, where disposable workers have long been a way of life. (Even in Japan, home of so-called lifetime jobs, it has been estimated that at least 75 percent of all workers are in fact subject to dismissal at the discretion of their employers.) And every year, the competition has come from a new quarter—steel, autos, textiles, cameras, and even computer chips. Not knowing from where the next onslaught would come, and desperately seeking ways to achieve the flexibility needed to react to their overseas competition, American firms seem to have found at least part of the answer in contingent workers. With the 1990s clearly the decade of global integration, disposable workers may become even more valuable.

Even once we understand the reasons *why* contingent workers are growing in number, there remains another significant question: what are their long-term implications? Critics argue that the lack of commitments inherent in contingent employment reduces worker loyalty to employers, engendering an "I don't care" attitude. And if workers don't care about the long–term survival of the company for which they are working, why should they worry about the quality of goods they produce? After all, if shoddy work ultimately causes the firm to go out of business, the worker simply can move to another "disposable job." Critics also note that the transient nature of many employment relationships discourages investment in training by workers and employers alike—because neither knows when the other may terminate the relationship. This tends to dampen long-term productivity improvement and wage growth. Thus, critics say, in the long run we may find ourselves unable to compete in high-technology industries, *and* end up with a large class of second-class workers mired in low-paying jobs with no hope of advancement.

Proponents of contingent-worker arrangements counter along three fronts. First, they note that some companies moved to the use of subcontractors and leased employees to escape work rules and other restrictions placed on them by unions or legislatures. As for quality control, proponents say, subcontractors and employee-leasing firms are picking up much of the burden. After all, Kelly Services—providers of temporary employees for periods as short as a day—has had decades of success in providing the "ultimate" in disposable (and relatively high-quality) workers. Finally, proponents note that the spread of part-time or transient jobs offering relatively lower pay and benefits is closely tied to the major changes in work-force composition over the last two decades. As newer entrants develop long-term attachments to the labor force, they and employers will have enhanced incentives to ensure that they move into jobs offering better pay and benefits and enhanced security and productivity.

Lacking a crystal ball, we can't know for sure what the long-term future or implications of contingent employment contracts will be. For now, perhaps the best measure may be found in the experience of Carlynn Hobbs, who works at home computing insurance premiums. Because she can set her own hours, Hobbs is able to tailor her schedule to the needs of her two young sons. And although higher pay and benefits would be nice, Hobbs nevertheless concludes that: "I'm fortunate to have found this job."

DISCUSSION QUESTIONS

1. Is it possible that some individuals have been forced into being contingent workers? What would happen to these people if they were prohibited from accepting such jobs?

2. If contingent workers get less training than they would as permanent employees, does this mean our workforce will end up with fewer skills than are needed to compete in international markets?

3. A larger proportion of high school graduates go on to college than was the case, say, 30 years ago. How would this affect the market for disposable workers?

4. How would growth of two-earner families affect the popularity of disposable-worker arrangements?

17

Million Dollar Men

There was a time when the sports page focused on batting averages, passing proficiency, and field-goal shooting. In recent years, however, many of the stories seem to be about salary caps, free agency, TV contracts and—most of all—money, big money.

Measured in today's dollars, Hall of Fame baseball player Ty Cobb earned $155,000 per year at the peak of his performance. Today, the *minimum* annual salary in major league baseball is $109,000. The top-paid baseball player earns $6.3 million per year, nine times the current dollar value of what Babe Ruth earned in 1930. Football quarterback John Elway a few years ago received a 153 percent salary increase in one year, bringing his pay to $4.8 million per season (about $300,000 per regular season game). In hockey and basketball, the story is much the same: top players pulling in salaries five and even ten times as large as the stars used to get paid.

The bucks don't stop with the players. Professional sports franchises are worth more than ever, despite their having to shell out $20 million (hockey) to $45 million (baseball) per year in salaries to keep league-leading teams playing. For example, the Baltimore Oriole baseball team sold for $12 million in 1979, changed hands in 1989 for $70 million, and was exchanged for $173 million in 1993. The Dallas Cowboys football franchise is estimated to be worth roughly $200 million. George Steinbrenner, owner of the New York Yankees, has a net worth estimated at $225 million. Much of this can be credited to the fact that Steinbrenner and his partners bought the Yankees for "only" $10 million; the team is now believed to have a market value in excess of $160 million.

Despite—or perhaps because of—the huge money involved in professional sports, teams and players in one league or another seem to be constantly battling with each other. There have been eight work stoppages in baseball over the last 25 years, and in 1994 both baseball and hockey players were simultaneously out on strike. The 1981 and 1987 professional football seasons were both marred by labor disputes. And in 1995, National Basketball Association players were locked out by team owners in a salary dispute.

At least part of the reason for the squabbles between players and owners over salaries has to do with some sharply different views of the nature of sporting competition at high levels. The conventional view has it that in each league, the owners are joined together in a **cartel**, agreeing among themselves not to compete for the services of individual players. In doing so, it is argued, the owners have been able to exercise **monopsony** power; by collectively acting as a single buyer of the players' services, the owners in each sport are able to force player salaries below what they otherwise would have been.

Owners have used a variety of arrangements to limit competition for players. For example, all of the major professional sports leagues use player "drafts." Although the specific rules of each draft differ, their general nature is quite simple. When a player becomes eligible to play a sport (after either high school or college, depending on the sport), he must subject himself to the draft before playing. Taking turns (with the worst teams picking first), each team selects players from the draft pool. Players must either play with the team that selects them or obtain permission from that team if they are to play with anyone else. In effect, the skills of each player are owned by the team that drafts him, and that team need not compete with any other team when deciding how much to pay the player.

A second important monopsony tool used by the owners has been an arrangement that in baseball was called the "reserve clause." Its operation has been similar across all professional sports and also at the college level among members of the National Collegiate Athletic Association (NCAA). Once a player began his professional career, the team for which he played could "reserve" the rights to the player each time his contract expired. Thus, even if another team was willing to pay the player a higher salary, the player was not free to move without the permission of his current team.

The reserve clause has been either eliminated or considerably watered down in most professional sports, a fact that has been partly responsible for the explosion in player salaries over the past 20 years. For example, the reserve clause was eliminated in 1976 in baseball. Measured in today's dollars, average baseball salaries have risen to $1.2 million from their previous level of about $120,000 per year.

Of course part of this increase in salaries has been caused by the rapidly growing popularity of professional sports, rather than by the added competition for players. Nevertheless, it is clear that restrictions on competition have played a key role in keeping player salaries down. For example, a relatively minor 1989 change in the rules governing competition among football owners produced an immediate jump of 30 percent in player salaries. It was another modest easing of the rules in 1993 that yielded the 153 percent raise for John Elway that we mentioned earlier.

Even in college sports, restrictions on competition seem to play a major role in determining what players are "paid." The NCAA reduces competition among its member schools by making players ineligible if they transfer to another NCAA college. Moreover, payments to players, other than scholarships and a minimal outside income, are banned. The result is that the total compensation that a player may receive typically ranges between $5000 and $20,000 per year. For many athletes, this is likely to be about the **marginal revenue product** that they generate. But for stars, amounts such as this are likely well below their market value. Indeed, according to one estimate, a professional-caliber football player (i.e., one good enough to be drafted) is worth over $500,000 per year in additional revenue to the school for whom he plays. Over a four-year career, a star player thus generates $2 million more in revenue than his college is allowed to compensate him under NCAA rules.[1]

Team owners (and college athletic directors) would likely object to our argument that the draft, the reserve clause, and so forth are merely monopsonistic devices that lower the wealth of players. They might (and indeed some do) argue that rules like these are necessary to ensure an even distribution of good players among all

---

[1] Robert W. Brown, "An Estimate of the Rent Generated by a Premium College Football Player," *Economic Inquiry*, Vol. 31, October 1993, pp. 671–84.

teams. Without the reserve rules and draft, it is said, clubs in larger markets would bid away the best talent. Games would be lopsided and bored spectators would quit buying tickets.

This reasoning seems plausible, but we must remember that *any* industry could make the same contention. For example, according to this argument, universities in New York, Chicago, and Los Angeles should be able to buy up all of the best professors and thus make the education "game" lopsided. In fact, of course, universities in small-market towns such as Palo Alto (Stanford), Ithaca (Cornell), and New Haven (Yale) manage to do quite well, as do competing universities in many other towns and cities across the country.

A more sophisticated argument in favor of the restrictive practices engaged in by sports teams goes like this: It is said that a team's or athlete's output is measured not by *absolute* skill but by *relative* performance—how well the team or player does against competitors. If this is true, then when a team drafts a better player out of college, although its own fans are better off, fans of other teams suffer. As a result, each team has too much incentive to hire good players and each player has too much incentive to improve his own skills, where "too much" means relative to the efficient level.

According to this reasoning, the situation in sports is much like that facing the owners of "view" properties along a magnificent coastline or overlooking some other beautiful vista. Each owner has an incentive to build a tall home to maximize the view he or she can consume. But doing so blocks the view of other owners, thereby reducing their enjoyment. Under such circumstances, the allocation of resources can be made more efficient if the owners agree to restrict competition among themselves. In the case of the view properties, this can involve limits on building heights and requirements that trees be trimmed regularly. In the case of sports, the limits can come in terms of the draft, the reserve clause, and other rules such as restrictions on team size.

Although there is disagreement over whether or not restrictive practices in sport are purely monopsonistic, there is little disagreement that professional athletes are worth a lot of money. Indeed, as the New York Yankees' owner noted, "You measure the value of a ballplayer by the number of fannies he puts in the seats." As long as the fans keep coming to the games, professional athletes will be handsomely paid—and they and the owners will likely still be arguing over just how handsomely that should be.

DISCUSSION QUESTIONS

1. On three occasions, rival leagues have emerged to compete with the National Football League. What do you think has happened to player salaries each time?

2. Football and basketball have instituted a "salary cap" that limits the total amount of money that a team may spend each year on player salaries. What effect would this have on average salaries?

3. If you were a team owner, how could you avoid the salary cap?

4. One way teams can compete with players is to offer them longer contracts or to guarantee contracts so players are paid whether they play or not. How do arrangements such as these affect the incentives of players to perform once they have signed the contract?

18

The Effects of the Minimum Wage

Ask workers if they would like a raise and the answer is likely to be a resounding yes. But ask them if they would like to be fired or have their hours of work reduced and they would probably tell you no. The effects of the minimum wage are centered on exactly these points.

Proponents of the **minimum wage**—the lowest hourly wage firms may legally pay their workers—argue that low-income workers are underpaid and unable to support themselves or their families. The minimum wage, they say, raises earnings at the bottom end of the wage distribution, with little or no disruption to workers or businesses. Opponents claim that most low-wage workers are low-skilled youths without families to support. The minimum wage, it is said, merely enriches a few teenagers at the far greater expense of many others, who can't get jobs. Most important, opponents argue, is that many individuals at the bottom end of the economic ladder lack the skills needed for employers to hire them at the current federal minimum of $4.25 per hour. Willing to work but unable to find jobs, these individuals never learn the basic on-the-job skills needed to move up the economic ladder to higher paying jobs. The issues are clear—but what are the facts?

The federal minimum wage was instituted in 1938 as a provision of the Fair Labor Standards Act (FLSA). It was originally set at $0.25 per hour, about 40 percent of the average manufacturing wage at the time. Over the next forty years, the legal minimum was raised periodically, roughly in accord with the movement of market wages throughout the economy. Typically, its level has averaged between

40 percent and 50 percent of average manufacturing wages. In response to the high inflation of the late 1970s, the minimum wage was hiked seven times between 1974 and 1981, reaching $3.35 per hour—about 42 percent of manufacturing wages. Ronald Reagan vowed to keep a lid on the minimum wage, and by the time he stepped down as president, the minimum's unchanged level left it at 31 percent of average wages. In 1989, after vetoing a hike in the minimum wage to $4.55 per hour, President Bush signed legislation that raised the minimum to $3.80 in 1990 and $4.25 in 1991. Four years later, President Clinton proposed raising it again, to $5.00 per hour.

About 2.5 million workers, less than 5 percent of the hourly wage earners in the United States, earn the minimum wage; another 1.7 million take home even less because the law doesn't cover them. Supporters of the minimum wage argue that it prevents exploitation of employees and helps them earn enough to support their families and themselves. Even so, a full-time minimum wage worker earns only $8500 a year, less than 60 percent of what the government considers enough to keep a family of four out of poverty. In fact, to get a family of four with one wage earner up to the poverty line, the minimum wage would have to be over $7.50 per hour.

Yet those who oppose the minimum wage argue that such calculations are irrelevant. For example, two-thirds of the workers earning the minimum wage are single, and they earn enough to put them *above* the poverty cutoff. Moreover, about half of these single workers are teenagers, most of whom have no financial obligations, except possibly for their clothing and car insurance expenditures. Thus, opponents argue that the minimum wage chiefly benefits upper-middle class teens who are least in need of assistance, at the same time that it costs the jobs of thousands of disadvantaged minority youths.

A few researchers—for example, Professor David Card of Princeton—dispute the contention that the minimum wage costs some individuals their jobs. Nevertheless, the overwhelming evidence on this issue points to a negative impact of the minimum wage on employment. After all, the number of workers demanded, like the quantity demanded for all goods, responds to price: the higher the price, the lower the number desired. There *is*, however, general debate over *how many* jobs are lost due to the minimum wage. For example, when the minimum wage was raised from $3.35 to $4.25, credible estimates of the number potential job losses ranged from 50,000 all the way up to 400,000. When President Clinton proposed raising the minimum to $5.00, researchers suggested that at least 100,000 jobs were at stake. With a workforce of 130 million persons, numbers like these may not sound very large. But most of the people who don't have jobs as a result of the minimum wage are teenagers; they comprise only about 5 percent of the workforce, but bear almost all of the burden of foregone employment alternatives.

Significantly, the youths most likely to lose work as a result of the minimum wage are disadvantaged teenagers, primarily minorities. On average, these teens enter the work force with the fewest job skills and the greatest need for on-the-job training. Until and unless these disadvantaged teenagers are allowed to acquire these skills, they are the most likely to be unemployed as a result of the minimum wage—and thus least likely to have the opportunity to move up the economic ladder. With a teen unemployment rate better than triple the overall rate, and unemployment among black youngsters hovering above 30 percent, critics argue that the minimum wage is a major impediment to long-term labor market success for minority youth.

Indeed, the minimum wage has an aspect that not many of its supporters are inclined to discuss: it can make employers more inclined to discriminate on the basis of sex or race. When wages are determined by market forces, employers who would discriminate on the basis of sex or race face a reduced, and thus more expensive, pool of workers. But when the government mandates an above-market wage, a surplus of low-skilled workers results, and it becomes easier and cheaper to discriminate. As Professor Lawrence Summers of Harvard University notes, the minimum wage "removes the economic penalty to the employer. He can choose the one who's white with blond hair."

Critics of the minimum wage also argue that it makes firms less willing to train workers lacking basic skills. Instead, companies may choose to hire only experienced workers whose abilities justify the higher wage. Firms are also likely to become less generous with fringe benefits in an effort to hold down labor costs. The prospect of more discrimination, less job training for low-skilled workers, and fewer fringe benefits for entry-level workers leaves many observers uncomfortable. As economist Jacob Mincer of Columbia

University notes, the minimum wage means "a loss of opportunity" for the hard-core unemployed.

The last time Congress and the President agreed to raise the minimum wage, it was only after a heated battle lasting ten months. Given the stakes involved—an improved standard of living for some, a loss of job opportunities for others—it is not surprising that discussions of the minimum wage soon turn to controversy. As one former high-level U.S. Department of Labor official has said: "When it comes to the minimum wage, there are no easy positions to take. Either you are in favor of more jobs, less discrimination, and more on-the-job training, or you support better wages for workers. Whatever stance you choose, you are bound to get clobbered by the opposition." And whenever the Congress and the President face this issue, one or both parties usually feel the same way.

DISCUSSION QUESTIONS

1. Are teenagers better off when a higher minimum wage enables some to get higher wages, but causes other to lose their jobs?

2. Are there methods other than a higher minimum wage that could raise the incomes of low-wage workers without reducing employment among minority youngsters?

3. Why do you suppose that organized labor groups, such as unions, are consistent supporters of a higher minimum wage, despite the fact that their members all earn much more than the minimum wage?

4. Is it possible that a higher minimum wage could ever *raise* employment?

Part Five

Political Economy

INTRODUCTION

The chief focus of economics has always been on explaining the behavior of the private sector. Yet dating back at least to the publication of Adam Smith's *Wealth of Nations* more than 200 years ago, economists have never missed an opportunity to apply their theories to additional realms of behavior. For the past 30 years or so, much of this effort has been devoted to developing theories that explain the actions of governments, as well as the consequences of those actions. This undertaking is often referred to as the study of political economy, for it often involves a mixture of politics and economics. As the selections in this section hint, economists do not yet have a unified theory of government. Nevertheless, they are making progress, and are sometimes able to offer surprising insights.

One of the first things that economists had to learn about government decision-making is that the costs of government policies are always higher than promised, and the benefits are always lower. This simple proposition forms the centerpiece of Chapter 19, "Foreign or Domestic? Ask A Bureaucrat," which explores the implications of federal rules that specify the minimum fuel efficiency permitted for new cars sold in the United States. Sometimes the effects of the federal regulations are at least mildly amusing—as they are when they induce an automaker to *fly* automobiles back and forth across the Atlantic in specially equipped airplanes in order to comply with federal "fuel economy" rules. Sometimes the effects are at least moderately expensive—as they are when they induce companies to spend millions of dollars redesigning cars, not to make them more fuel efficient, but solely to satisfy the peculiar accounting conventions of the regulations. And sadly, sometimes the effects of the regulations are tragic: Indeed, reliable estimates suggest that the federal fuel economy standards have forced automakers to downsize their cars to such an extent as to make them less crash-worthy. It is estimated that 3000

Americans lose their lives in traffic accidents every year as a result of these particular regulations.

In Chapter 20, "Education and Choice," we examine the implications of government operation of the means of production, where the output produced is education in public schools. There is growing evidence that the quality of education produced by our school system has been declining over the past 30 years, and that a principal reason for this is the government's effective monopoly in the provision of primary and secondary education. One solution to this problem would be to turn primary and secondary education over to the private sector, perhaps accompanied by government-provided education vouchers that low- and middle income families could use to finance the education they want for their children. Realistically, this solution is probably not politically viable, so this chapter examines another alternative: forcing public schools to compete with one another by permitting children to go to whatever public schools they choose. Based on the evidence from those areas of the country that have experimented with such an arrangement, it appears that the likely result would be a marked improvement in the quality of primary and secondary education in the United States, with no increase in spending required to achieve it. It seems that competition works wonders in government, just as it does in the private sector.

Human life is precious. Few would disagree with this, but many might argue over the lengths to which we should go to protect it. In Chapter 21, "An Eye for an Eye," we address an issue that dates back at least to Biblical times: capital punishment. Although economics cannot tell us whether murderers *should* be executed for their crimes, it can shed some light on what happens when they *are* executed. We find that the "demand" for murder (on the part of the perpetrators) is much like the demand for other things: It obeys the law of demand. When murder is made more costly, fewer murders are committed. Because capital punishment increases the cost of committing murder, this means that implementing the death penalty reduces the number of murders. Executing a murderer may save the lives of numerous would-be victims. Does this mean that capital punishment is good public policy? Not even economics can answer that question—although a better understanding of the economic issues involved may help you decide if capital punishment should be public policy.

One of the messages that keeps cropping up when economists take a close look at social and economic policies is that good inten-

tions often lead to unanticipated and—too often—harmful consequences. As we see in Chapter 22, "Poverty in America," for more
than 30 years, U.S. policy makers and politicians have been trying to
"do something" about poverty. Thus far they have managed to spend
many hundreds of billions of dollars on the problem without bringing
about much of a reduction in the extent of poverty. The good news is
that the expansion of Social Security and Medicare have transformed
the elderly from one of the poorest groups in U.S. society to one of its
most affluent. The bad news is that a host of other government programs have helped create an entirely new class among the poor—single-parent families. The evidence is clear that simply "throwing
money" at the problem will not solve it in any meaningful sense. But
it is not clear what—if anything—will bring about a lasting reduction
in the extent of poverty in the United States. The choice may then
come down to deciding which policies offer the lowest-cost means of
achieving the modest improvements that are possible.

Our final foray into political economy, Chapter 23, "Where
There's Smoking, There's Fire," offers a glimpse at how three different levels of government—federal, state, and local—choose to deal
with the same behavior: tobacco smoking. The act of smoking is not
only demonstrably harmful to those individuals who engage in it, but
it also creates a **negative externality** for other individuals in their
proximity. In principle, one might expect a government acting in the
interests of economic efficiency to tax or otherwise regulate smoking
so as to reduce the damage inflicted by smokers on nonsmokers.
Although the federal government's behavior is not entirely consistent with this prediction (for it goes to great lengths to implicitly sub-
sidize tobacco farmers), there is little doubt that state and local governments are moving rapidly to implement regulations that reduce
the damages that smokers may inflict on bystanders. This finding is
particularly interesting, because the ability of individuals to move
freely among state and local jurisdictions means these legal authorities each face more **competition** than does the federal government.
As we saw in our examination of education, competition produces increased efficiency in government, just as it does in the private sector.
Thomas Jefferson told us, "that government is best which governs
least." An economist might well add: "especially when it is forced to
compete the most."

19

Foreign or Domestic? Ask a Bureaucrat

> Things are not always what they seem
> Phaedrus,
> circa A.D. 8

If there were a Murphy's Law of economic policy-making, it would be this: *The costs are always higher than promised, and the benefits are always lower.* The federal law that regulates automobile fuel economy provides just one example of this fundamental principle, and along the way demonstrates that what Phaedrus had to say 2000 years ago is true today.

Our story begins in the 1970s, when the United States was in the middle of the so-called energy crisis. The Organization of Petroleum Exporting Countries (OPEC), a cartel of major oil-producing countries, had succeeded in causing the prices of petroleum products (including gasoline) to rise to record-high levels. Consumers reacted by conserving on their use of gasoline and other petroleum products, and Congress responded by enacting legislation mandating energy conservation as the law of the land. One of these laws, known as the corporate average fuel economy (CAFE) standard, requires that each auto manufacturer's passenger cars sold in this country meet a federally mandated fuel economy standard. The 1995 new car fleets, for example, had to average 27.5 miles per gallon of gasoline. If an automaker sells a gas-guzzler that gets only 15 mpg, somewhere along the line it must also sell enough gas-sipping subcompacts so that the average fuel economy of the entire fleet of cars sold by the company works out to 27.5 miles per gallon (mpg). If an automaker's average fuel economy is worse than 27.5 mpg, the corporation is fined $50 per car for each 0.1 mile per gallon it falls short. For example, if General Motors were to fail to meet the CAFE standard by only one mile per gallon, it could be subject to penalties of $200 million per year or more.

One obvious way for a manufacturer to comply with the CAFE standard would be to import boatloads of high-mileage cars from Japan or Europe to increase the overall measured fuel economy of the cars it sells. To discourage this, the law divides manufacturers' overall sales into domestic and imported fleets, and dictates that each fleet must meet the CAFE standard. An automobile that has 75 percent or more of its components made in the United States or Canada is considered domestic, while a car with less than that is foreign (i.e., imported). By requiring that both domestically produced and foreign-made cars meet the same standard, Congress hoped to be able to force U.S. automakers to upgrade the mileage of their traditional domestic cars. It was argued that this would not only enhance fuel economy, but it would also protect the auto industry jobs of the U.S. workers who made those cars. In fact, the law may well have reduced employment in the U.S. auto industry. Just as importantly, the CAFE standard has forced automobile manufacturers to play costly games in their efforts to meet the standards, and has resulted in higher costs for consumers as well.

The CAFE standard was first introduced at a time when the price of gasoline, measured in terms of today's dollars, was about $3 per gallon. During the mid-1980s, price-cutting by members of the OPEC cartel, combined with a rise in oil production elsewhere, sent gasoline prices into free fall. By 1995, with gasoline less than half as expensive (in inflation-adjusted dollars) as it was in the 1970s, the legally mandated CAFE standard of 27.5 mpg almost certainly resulted in cars that didn't consume *enough* gasoline. This seems like a strange conclusion, so we want to be sure we understand why it is correct.

There is no doubt that conserving gasoline is a good thing, for gasoline is a **scarce good.** If we are able to accomplish the same objectives (such as making a trip to the grocery store) and use less gasoline in doing so, the money that would have been spent on the gas can now be spent on other goods. Yet conserving gasoline is itself a costly activity. In the extreme case, we could engage in 100 percent conservation of gasoline, but doing so would mean giving up automobiles altogether! Somewhat more realistically, reducing the amount of gasoline that cars burn requires that they be lighter, have smaller engines, and be smaller and sometimes less crash-resistant. To meet the CAFE standards, for example, automobile manufacturers have had to switch to production techniques that are more costly, use materials (such as aluminum and high-tech plastics) that are more easily damaged in accidents and more costly to repair, and design engines that are less responsive and more difficult and costly to keep in proper running order. Although these are all things that probably would make sense if the price of gas were $3 per gallon, many economists believe that at $1.50 per gallon the principal effect of the CAFE standard is to raise consumers' total transportation costs: The costs of conserving on gasoline exceed the savings from consuming less of it.

The fuel economy law has also produced some otherwise inexplicable behavior on the part of the automobile manufacturers. Consider the Cadillac Allanté, produced by General Motors until recently. Although the car was assembled in Michigan, the body was fabricated in Italy. As the federal bureaucrats reckoned things, only 55 percent of the Allanté was domestic, so it counted as a foreign car. This was good for GM, because the Allanté's low gas mileage (20.5 mpg) got charged against GM's otherwise fuel stingy import fleet, rather than against its domestic account. Keeping the Allanté classified as a foreign car was not cheap, however, for the car's parts had to be flown back and forth across the Atlantic in a specially-equipped Boeing 747. Partly as a result, despite the car's $60,000 price tag, GM lost money on the Allanté. If GM had tried to cut costs by making the Allanté entirely in the United States, the addition of another low-mileage car to the company's domestic fleet could have cost the company millions of dollars in federal penalties for violating the CAFE standard. Finally, GM simply gave up and stopped producing the Allanté.

Consider also the Ford Crown Victoria, a full-size sedan that has long been a favorite with state and local police forces and with middle-aged, middle-income Americans. The Crown Victoria and its sister car, the Mercury Grand Marquis, exemplify the classic domestically produced gas-guzzler that the United States grew up on. Yet in 1992 Ford was faced with the prospects of big penalties for selling too many low-mileage, large cars. Instead of discontinuing production of the Crown Victoria and Grand Marquis, Ford chose to reduce the "domestic content" of the cars (the amount that is U.S.- or Canadian-made) from 94 percent to 73 percent, enabling it to classify both vehicles as foreign rather than domestic. It accomplished this trick by buying eight high-value components outside the United

States. The cars still got only 24 mpg, but because they had shock absorbers from Japan, key engine parts from Spain, brake components from Germany, axle parts from Britain, and windshields, instrument panels, and fuel tanks from Mexico, federal bureaucrats classified the Crown Victoria and Grand Marquis as imported cars. The U.S. workers who used to supply these parts to Ford are presumably looking for work elsewhere; meanwhile, the "imported" Crown Victoria and Mercury Marquis had their low fuel economy offset by the 45-mpg Festiva, which Ford built and brought in from Korea.

Japanese automakers have the same incentive as U.S. manufacturers to limit domestic content in order to keep cars with relatively poor mileage in their import fleet. Some Honda Accord models, for example, average only 26 mpg. Honda makes most of its Accords in the United States and would risk federal CAFE penalties if the Accord were classified as a domestic car. To avoid this, Honda holds U.S. production down and imports extra Accords from Japan so that the overall U.S. content of Accords as a class falls well below 75 percent. Legally, that makes *all* Accords part of Honda's imported car fleet, so the Accord's relatively poor gas mileage can be averaged in with that of the made-in-Japan CRX, which gets as much as 59 mpg. The result is fewer automobiles made in the United States, but no federal penalties for Honda.

Sometimes it takes a degree in accounting to figure out a car's nationality. For example, when determining the domestic content of an item for the purposes of the fuel economy law, *all* of the costs associated with the manufacture of the item must be taken into account. That certainly seems reasonable. But consider this: 75 percent of the parts for the Toyota Camry engine are made in Japan, yet the engine is legally classified as "made in America." Why? Because the parts are assembled in Toyota's Kentucky plant, and all of the plant's labor, overhead, distribution, and profits are considered when determining whether an item is domestic or foreign. (Beginning with the 1995 model year cars, auto makers had to reveal the "domestic content" of their cars on a window sticker. But the legislation mandating content labeling *excludes* labor, unlike the CAFE standard, which includes it. So the Honda Accord, for example, which is labeled as 50 percent "domestic" is actually closer to 65 percent. And, because "domestic" includes Canada, some numbers are even stranger than this. For example, the Camaro, labeled 91 percent, is actually built in Quebec, while the 50 percent Honda Civic hails from East Liberty, Ohio.)

It is a strange law indeed that transforms a full-sized Ford into an "import" and supposedly protects the jobs of U.S. autoworkers by inducing Honda to import more cars from Japan. Yet more often than not, costly oddities such as these are the consequence when the government tries to micromanage the decision making of firms and consumers. It is almost impossible for legislators and bureaucrats to know all of the ins and outs of a business. As a result, a seemingly innocuous rule can distort choices in unforeseen—and sometimes tragic—ways. The seemingly obvious way to respond to a law that requires enhanced fuel efficiency is to redesign engines so that they burn less fuel. But another highly effective means of reducing the fuel appetite of automobiles is to "downsize" them by making them smaller and lighter. One recent study by Robert Crandall of the Brookings Institution and John Graham of Harvard found that the CAFE standard has forced automakers to produce cars that are about 500 pounds lighter than they would have been without the law. A 500-pound weight reduction implies a 14 percent increase in the fatality risk for the occupants of a car involved in an accident. That translates into approximately 3000 additional deaths per year, plus another 15,000 or so "serious nonfatal injuries" each year. Surely Congress did not intend to add to highway mayhem by passing the CAFE standard, yet that has been one of the consequences.

Micromanagement by the government also produces strange (and wasteful) results because legislative and bureaucratic decision-making often cannot keep up with the changing dynamics of the marketplace. The decisions that consumers and firms make are always dependent on input and output prices: when those prices change, so do the decisions. The CAFE standard was originally implemented when inflation-adjusted gasoline prices were twice as high as they are today. In the case of the Crown Victoria, for example, if gasoline were $3 per gallon, Ford probably would have redesigned the car to improve its gas mileage. But with gas at only $1.50 per gallon or less, it made more sense for Ford simply to reduce the domestic content of the car to avoid facing stiff legal penalties. As a result, there was no improvement in the car's fuel efficiency, consumers ended up paying a higher price for a lower-quality car, and some U.S. workers who would have helped build the Crown Victoria had to look for jobs elsewhere. It's hard to believe that this is what Congress intended, but it is a good example of the fact that when it comes to economic policy-making, the costs are always higher than promised, and the benefits are always lower.

DISCUSSION QUESTIONS

1. Why do you think Congress passed the CAFE standard?

2. Does your answer to the previous question imply that either (1) consumers do not know what is in their own best interest, or (2) firms will not voluntarily provide the goods (including fuel economy) that consumers want to purchase?

3. Suppose that Congress really knows what the best average fuel economy for automobiles is. How do you think "best" is (or should be) defined? Do the costs and benefits of achieving a particular level of fuel economy play a role in determining that definition?

4. If Congress wanted to increase the average fuel economy of cars, could it accomplish this by imposing a tax on gasoline? What are the advantages and disadvantages of using taxes rather than standards to achieve an improvement in fuel economy?

20

Education and Choice

In 1974, East Harlem ranked thirty-second among New York City's 32 community school districts. Only 15 percent of its students read at or above grade level. By 1989 this inner-city school district ranked sixteenth, and more than 65 percent of its students read at or above grade level. By the mid-1990s, the East Harlem district—located in one of the poorest areas of New York—was still improving and had a *waiting list* of teachers wishing to work there. What happened in East Harlem? A massive infusion of federal funds to promote educational reform? A multiyear grant from a major charitable foundation? Perhaps an influx of upscale, yuppie parents demanding educational excellence? The answer: none of the above. What happened in East Harlem can be summarized by just one word: *choice.*

In 1974 the administrators of the East Harlem school district, faced with a school system that had nowhere to go but up, made a radical move: They decided to permit choice in their district. Teachers and schools were permitted to choose curricula and programs they thought would provide the best educational products, and students and parents were allowed to choose from among those products the ones best suited to their preferences and educational objectives. Along the way, mistakes were made and lessons learned. Some schools did a poor job, failed to attract "new customers," and have closed their doors. Other schools provided popular, effective programs that have been replicated successfully elsewhere in the district. Overall, the quality of education in East Harlem improved beyond even the most optimistic expectations of 1974. Indeed, the improvement was so great that the East

Harlem educators decided to enter a new "market." The district had been administering education through the eighth grade only; in 1985 it assumed responsibility for a neighborhood high school with a graduation rate of 7 percent. Although the school accepts any student who wants to attend, its graduation rate now exceeds 90 percent, and almost all of its graduates go on to some kind of post-secondary education.

The freedom of choice offered schools, teachers, parents, and students in the East Harlem school district is unusual in public school systems today, but so is the success of East Harlem schools. In most school districts, the curriculum and course offerings for each grade level are decided upon from "on high"—at the level of the district or the state administrator. Once it is decided that chemistry and biology but not geology are to be offered in high schools, all high schools in the district typically must abide by that decision. Moreover, all individuals teaching chemistry generally must follow the approved study plan and use the approved book for that course without regard for the talents or interests of the particular teachers. The choices available to the "consumers" of education—students and their parents—are equally circumscribed. Once they have chosen a place to live, they are stuck with the particular set of schools, elementary through secondary, to which they are assigned by the district. If high school *A* offers advanced placement chemistry and high school *B* does not, then students assigned to high school *B* simply will not have the option of taking advanced placement chemistry in the public school system.

In important respects, then, each school district and each school within a district is much like a **monopolist,** albeit on a small scale. If the customers (students and their parents) of a district are dissatisfied with the quality, type, or amount of product being offered, they cannot—short of physically moving—choose to consume the services of another public school district. Similarly, if students or parents are dissatisfied with their assigned school within a district, they cannot choose a competing public school within the district.

Parents and students can attempt to alter district or school policies by writing letters, voicing their opinions in school board or PTA meetings, or engaging in political activities. Yet if they are in the minority by even one vote, they are stuck with the preferences of the majority. It is also true that people can "vote with their feet" by relocating their residences to another school district or by utilizing the services of private schools. Yet such measures are very costly and generally are taken only by persons who are either extremely dissatisfied or extremely wealthy. Few rational people are willing to sustain the cost and inconvenience of selling one house and buying another simply to enjoy a school system that is a little better—particularly because they will have so little voice in the operation of the *new* school system once they have chosen it. For those people opting for private schools, there is a double burden to bear: In addition to the bills for private school tuition, they must continue paying taxes to support the public school system they find unsatisfactory! All in all, public schools are largely insulated from competition.

This situation is in sharp contrast to the market for magazines, for example; like schools, magazines are a source of knowledge and (for some) entertainment. Consider *Time* magazine, which is headquartered in Manhattan, a borough of New York City. Taxes are not levied on the residents of Manhattan to cover the costs of publishing *Time*, and one need not be a resident of Manhattan to read it; residents of Brooklyn, East Harlem, and even Honolulu are free to read it should they choose to pay for it. If the owners of *Time* produce a high-quality product at a reasonable price, readership will grow and the owners of the magazine will become wealthy (presumably the reason the owners are in business). If the owners produce a shoddy product or charge a price that is too high, consumers can and will switch to any one of numerous competing news magazines, thereby reducing the wealth of the owners of *Time*. In either event, competition among magazines yields diversity of choice and the provision of high-quality products at reasonable prices.

We have already noted how the relative lack of competition among public schools restricts the choices available to parents and students. Many experts also believe that the monopolistic position of public schools has contributed to inferior primary and secondary education in the United States relative to other comparable nations, and to a significant decline in educational quality in the United States over the past quarter-century.

It has long been recognized that when U.S. students are exposed to educational systems in other industrialized nations, they are commonly at least a grade level behind the other students in those countries, even in standard subjects such as mathematics. Recent research has systematically confirmed this observation. One major study found that the *average* Japanese student outscores the top 5 percent of U.S. students enrolled in college-prep math courses. Other research has revealed that in chemistry and physics, advanced science students in U.S. high schools perform worse than their counterparts in almost all countries studied. In biology, U.S. students ranked dead last, behind such nations as Singapore and Thailand.

The superior performance of foreign high school students can be explained in part by the fact that many foreign nations place more emphasis on training at the primary and secondary school levels, and less emphasis on college-level training. Nevertheless, it is telling that competition is the rule among school systems in most other developed nations. The French, for example, have two parallel systems above the elementary grades, a public one and a Catholic one, both paid for out of taxes. The Italian system is similar. In Japan, schools are graded by the performance of their students on the university entrance exams, and teachers in high-ranking schools are promoted and paid accordingly. Many observers agree that the lack of competitive pressure among public school systems in this country has largely robbed U.S. schools of the incentive to excel. Even the president of the American Federation of Teachers has acknowledged the deficiency in U.S. schools: "Only about 5 percent of our graduates leave high school prepared to do what is considered real college-level work. . . . The overwhelming majority of American students who go on to higher education will be learning in college what their European colleagues learned in high school or even junior high school."

There is little doubt that the quality of education in American school systems has deteriorated over the past quarter-century. Between 1963 and 1980, scores on the widely used Scholastic Aptitude Test (SAT) plunged 90 points; by 1994 they had recovered only about 10 points of that loss. Between 1972 and 1981 the number of high school seniors scoring above 600 (out of a possible 800) on the verbal portion of the SAT dropped 40 percent; by 1994 this remained nearly 30 percent below the 1972 figure. Although scores on the mathematics portion of the SAT have held up some-what better, this amounts to little more than stagnation in an area requiring significant improvement. A few years ago, the federally-funded National Assessment of Educational Progress (NAEP) found that, despite supposed efforts at "educational reform" in this country, the previous decade had witnessed improvements in mathematics skills that were "confined primarily to lower order skills." Indeed, the NAEP report concluded that only 6.4 percent of high school seniors have mastered "multi-step problem solving and algebra"—exactly the sort of skills essential to successful per-formance at the college level.[1]

What can be done about the sad state of primary and sec-ondary education in this country? Many observers argue that competition among schools, fostered by greater freedom of choice, is essential to any solution. The experiment of the East Harlem school district is one example of the power of choice in promoting excellence. On a much broader scale, a series of programs begun in the state of Minnesota are providing even more compelling evi-dence of the importance of choice.

In 1985 the governor of Minnesota proposed that juniors and seniors in public schools in the state be permitted to receive all or part of their last two years of high school in colleges or vocational schools, with state monies following them from high school to pay their tuition, lab fees, and book fees. The governor also recom-mended that families be allowed to send their children to public schools outside their home districts, as long as the receiving dis-tricts had room and the movement did not harm desegregation ef-forts. Despite vigorous opposition to the proposals by the teach-ers' unions, school boards, and superintendents' groups, four laws allowing greater freedom of educational choice have been passed in Minnesota, and the results are encouraging.

In the first five years of its operation, more than 10,000 students took advantage of the program permitting them to take college

---

[1] Consider, for example, the following question: "Which of the following is true of 87 percent of 10? (a) It is greater than 10. (b) It is less than 10. (c) It is equal to 10. (d) Can't tell?" The NAEP report concluded that all high school seniors should be able to answer this question correctly. In fact, only 51 percent were able to do so.

courses while still in high school, and many of them had higher grade point averages in those courses than the first-year college students. The program has attracted hundreds of students who had dropped out of high school due to boredom or frustration. Many participants are the first in their families to attend college. As one of these students put it, the program "changed my sense of what was possible."

Just as important, the program has stimulated many high schools to improve their own programs. For example, the number of advanced-placement courses offered by Minnesota high schools quadrupled—without any new mandates or dollars targeted for this purpose. More than 50 high schools have been encouraged to establish cooperative programs with colleges and universities that let them offer courses right in the high schools.

Under another Minnesota program, begun in 1987, students who do not succeed in one junior or senior high school are allowed to attend a school outside their district. Several thousand students have already taken advantage of this plan, about half of them school dropouts. Another law, which became effective in 1989, enables Minnesota students in all grades to attend school outside their districts, subject to space and racial balance considerations. By the mid-1990s, between 5 and 10 percent of all students each year were exercising their right to choose among public schools in Minnesota.

The East Harlem and Minnesota programs show that when choice among schools is permitted, the resulting competition improves the quality of education. Over the last few years, at least seven other states have followed Minnesota's lead, offering their students the option of attending school in a different district. Programs in these and other locales are reaffirming this conclusion: When students are given a choice of schools, graduation rates improve, student achievement increases, and parents are more involved and satisfied. Even teachers and school administrators—often initially fearful of the consequences of competition—are apparently finding that the opportunity to create new and distinctive programs offers rewards far outweighing the extra effort involved.

The famous golfer Arnold Palmer once remarked, "If you're not competing, you're dead." For America's moribund public school systems, the message from Minnesota, East Harlem, and elsewhere seems to be the converse: competition brings vitality. It is easy to imagine that today's students are hoping this message is being received as clearly as it is being transmitted.

DISCUSSION QUESTIONS

1. Who gains and who loses when there is more competition among public schools?

2. Some people have argued that we should institute educational vouchers that could be used by students to finance their education *either* in public schools or private schools of their choice. What are the advantages and disadvantages of such a scheme?

3. Why is most schooling in the United States operated by governments and paid for by taxpayers, rather than being privately provided and financed? Does your answer imply that most medical care, for example, should be provided by the government and paid for by taxpayers? Answer the same question regarding food, clothing, and shelter.

4. In general, most state universities charge lower tuition to "instate" students than to "out-of-state" students. The implicit subsidy to in-state students averages about $5000 per school year, but students may only take advantage of the subsidy if they stay in their home state—they cannot take a $5000 voucher with them to use at a college in another state. What would happen to competition among colleges if students could take their subsidies to whatever state they preferred? What is likely to happen to the quality of college education? Would you go to your state university if you could take your subsidy wherever you liked?

21

An Eye for an Eye

In 1994 the number of inmates in America's state and federal prisons topped one million for the first time. An additional 500,000 or so people were estimated to be in local jails. The growing numbers of people behind bars has made the United States second in the world, behind Russia, when it come to incarceration rates. Across the country, many local, state, and even federal prisons are packed with twice as many inmates as they were designed to house.[1] Some correctional systems in America are so crowded they are under court order to release prisoners as fast as they admit new ones—regardless of the consequences.

Today's crowded prisons are the result of two forces. First, the crime rate has been hovering at record levels since the mid-1970s. The chance that a household of four will be victimized by a serious crime in any given year is more than 20 percent—and rising.[1] Second, government authorities have become increasingly aware of the high costs that crimes impose on society, and have started toughening up law enforcement. The Federal Bureau of Investigation estimates that an average crime costs society about $2300. Because the typical professional criminal commits nearly 200 crimes per year, the annual costs imposed on society by such a person's crimes are $430,000. Many authorities now feel that the $25,000 to $40,000 a year it costs to keep a criminal in prison is beginning to look like a bargain. As a result, stepped-up law enforcement activities have doubled a criminal's chances of imprisonment over the last 15

---

[1] Serious crimes—called Part I crimes by the U.S. Department of Justice—include homicide, forcible rape, robbery, aggravated assault, burglary, larceny-theft, and motor vehicle theft.

years.[2] Despite the high and rising cost of crime—made worse by the rapid spread of drug trafficking over the last 15 years—many taxpayers are reluctant to incur the costs of building more prisons. This attitude stems partly from the fact that new prisons are expensive: Prison construction costs run from $50,000 to $100,000 per bed, plus, of course, the operating costs of keeping prisoners on a daily basis. Important, however, is that taxpayer reluctance to foot the bill stems from a sense of uncertainty about whether punishment really deters crimes. Do tougher penalties really discourage people from committing crimes? What sort of penalties are most effective? Should criminals be fined, imprisoned, put on probation, or perhaps simply executed? Does capital punishment *really* deter people from committing murder? To begin to answer such questions, we clearly must have some notion of the economic relationship between crime and punishment—or, perhaps more to the point, between punishment and crime.

There is one thing we can be sure of at the start: Uniformly heavy punishments for all crimes will lead to a relatively larger number of *major* crimes. Let's look at the reasoning. All decisions are made on the margin. If theft and murder will be punished by the same fate, there is no marginal deterrence to murder. If a theft of $5 is met with a punishment of 10 years in jail and a theft of $50,000 incurs the same sentence, why not go all the way and steal $50,000? There is no marginal deterrence against committing the bigger theft.

To establish deterrents that are correct at the margin, we must observe empirically how criminals respond to changes in punishments. This leads us to the question of how people decide whether to commit a "crime." A theory as to what determines the supply of criminal offenses needs to be established.

Adam Smith, the founder of modern economics, once said:

> The affluence of the rich excites the indignation of the poor, who are often both driven by want, and prompted by envy, to invade his possessions. It is only under the shelter of the civil magistrate that the owner of that valuable property, which is acquired by the labour of many years, or perhaps by many successive generations, can sleep a

---

[2] Despite this, a criminal is still significantly less likely to be imprisoned today than 35 years ago; between 1960 and 1975, the probability of being imprisoned for committing a crime fell from 6 percent to 2 percent.

single night in security. He is at all times surrounded by unknown enemies, whom, though he never provokes, he can never appease, and
from whose injustice he can be protected only by the powerful arm
of the civil magistrate continually held up to chastise it. The acquisi-
tion of valuable and extensive property, therefore, necessarily requires the establishment of civil government. Where there is no property, or at least none that exceeds the value of two or three days'
labour, civil government is not so necessary.[3]

Thus, Smith concluded, robberies will be committed in any society
in which one person has substantially more property than another.
If Smith is correct, we can surmise that the individuals who engage
in robberies are seeking income. We can also suppose that, before
acting, a criminal might be expected to look at the anticipated costs
and returns of criminal activity. These could then be compared with
the net returns from legitimate activities. In other words, those engaging in crimes may be thought of as doing so on the basis of a
cost-benefit analysis in which the benefits to them outweigh the
costs. The benefits of the crime of robbery are clear: loot. The costs
to the criminal would include, but not be limited to, apprehension
by the police, conviction, and jail. The criminal's calculations are
thus analogous to those made by an athlete when weighing the cost
of possible serious injury against the benefits to be gained from participating in a sport.

If we view the supply of offenses in this manner, we can come
up with ways in which society can lower the net expected benefit for
committing any illegal activity. That is, we can figure out how to reduce crime most effectively. Indeed, economists have applied this
sort of reasoning to study empirically the impact of punishment on
criminal activity. Time and again, they have found that (1) increasing the probability that criminals will be detected, apprehended, and
punished reduces the number of crimes committed; and (2) increasing the severity of the punishment has the same type of effect—the
supply of crimes is reduced. One implication of these findings is that
court-ordered early-release programs—which replace imprisonment with probation—can be expected to increase crime, particularly property crimes such as theft and burglary.

Can this theory be applied to a crime such as murder, and thus
assist in decisions about capital punishment? Sociologists, psycholo-

---

[3] Adam Smith, *The Wealth of Nations*, 1776.

gists, and others have numerous theories relating the number of murders committed to various psychological, sociological, and demographic variables. In general, they have stressed social and psychological factors as determinants of violent crime and have therefore felt that capital punishment would have no deterrent effect. Economists, on the other hand, have stressed a cost-benefit equation, which implies that capital punishment would deter violent crime.

We start with a commodity called the act of murder. If the act of murder is like any other commodity, the quantity "demanded" (by perpetrators, of course, not victims) will be negatively related to the relative price. But what is the price of murder? Ignoring the sociological, psychological, and psychic costs of murder, we must consider the probability of being caught and, after capture, the possible jail sentence or capital punishment that may be imposed. We must also keep in mind, however, the *probability* of the implementation of any particular penalty. Thus, it would do little good to observe the difference in murder rates between states that have capital punishment and states that do not. Instead, we must assess the probability of a convicted murderer's actually being *executed* in those states that have capital punishment, and compare this probability with what happens in states that do not. In some states that allow capital punishment, the probability of a convicted murderer's being executed is zero. We find, for example, that a charge of first-degree murder is often changed to a charge of second-degree murder if the penalty for first-degree murder is execution. In states that do not allow the death penalty, first-degree murder sentences are given more frequently. Because these variations exist among states, it is necessary to look at the actual number of executions within a state, and not merely the laws, in order to establish whether capital punishment is actually a deterrent to murder.

Critics of the economic analysis of crime immediately say that a typical murderer, either in a moment of unreasoned passion or when confronted with an unanticipated situation (for example, during an armed robbery), does not take into account the expected probability of lethal injection or a trip to the gas chamber. That is, murderers supposedly are not acting rationally when they murder. Is this a valid criticism of the economic model of the demand for murder? The answer is fundamentally an empirical issue, but the logic of such an argument is suspect. Indeed, if one contends that the expected cost of committing a murder has no effect on the quantity of murders, one is implicitly denying the **law of demand**, or stating that the **elasticity of demand** for murder is zero. One is also confusing the average murderer with the marginal murderer. All potential murderers do not have to react to the change in the expected cost of committing a murder for the economist's theory to be useful. If a sufficient number of marginal murderers act *as if* they were responding to the higher expected cost of murder, the **demand curve** for murders by perpetrators will be downward sloping.

A few economists have used economic models to study the demand for murder empirically. One of the first statistical studies of significance was that by Isaac Erlich.[4] One of the variables he included was the objective conditional risk of being executed if caught and convicted of murder. Erlich found that a 15 percent increase in the chance of being executed would reduce the number of murders by about 1 percent. The implication of these results, given the number of murders and executions in the period covered by the study (1935-1969) is striking. The implied trade-off between murders and executions was about 7 or 8 to 1. As Erlich put it, "an additional execution per year over the period of time in question may have resulted, on average, in 7 or 8 fewer murders." The deterrent effect of capital punishment on the crime of murder was more recently also analyzed by economist Stephen Layson, whose findings are even more suggestive. Layson concluded that every execution of a convicted murderer deters, on average, 18 other murders that would have occurred without it. He also studied the relationship between arrests and convictions of murderers and the murder rate. He found that a 1 percent increase in the arrest rate for murder would lead to 250 fewer murders per year and that a 1 percent increase in murder convictions would deter about 105 murders.

As might be expected, these findings are highly controversial and have led to an ongoing debate. For example, critics have stressed the tenuous statistical basis of the findings that fewer murders are committed when the chance of execution is higher. While the argument over capital punishment continues, the evidence that crime rates in general appear to vary inversely with estimates of penalties, probabilities of conviction, and legal opportunities has re-

---

[4] Isaac Erlich, "The Deterrent Effect of Capital Punishment: A Question of Life and Death," *The American Economic Review,* Vol. 65, no. 3, June 1975.

ceived substantial support. Yet the arrest rate for murders is 75 percent; only 38 percent of all murders result in a conviction, and less than 1 percent of murders result in execution. It is perhaps not too hard to understand why a substantial majority of Americans now favor the death penalty.

One final note. In the case of capital punishment, or any other punishment, deterrence requires that the penalty must be believed to fall on the guilty parties rather than to apply randomly. History tells us that under the emperors, executions in China were frequent. The emperors were not always so diligent, however, about executing the right person. Such a system of "punishment" does little good for society in terms of combating crime, not to mention the loss suffered by innocent victims and their families.

DISCUSSION QUESTIONS

1. The analysis just presented seems to make the assumption that criminals act rationally. Does the fact that they do not necessarily do so negate the analysis?

2. In many cases, murder is committed among people who know each other. Does this mean that raising the price the murderer must pay will not affect the quantity of murder demanded by perpetrators?

3. Consider the following prescription for punishments: "Eye for eye, tooth for tooth, hand for hand, foot for foot . . ." Suppose that our laws followed this rule, and further suppose that we spent enough money on law enforcement to apprehend everyone who broke the law. What would the crime rate be? (*Hint:* If the penalty for stealing $10 was $10, and if you were *certain* that you would be caught, would there be any expected gain from the theft? Would there be an expected gain from the theft if the penalty were only, say, $1?)

4. In recent years, the penalty for selling illegal drugs has been increased sharply. What does this do to the incentive to sell drugs? For the people who decide to sell drugs anyway, what do the higher penalties for dealing do to their incentive to commit *other* crimes (such as murder) while they are engaged in selling drugs?

22

Poverty in America

In 1965, the poorest 20 percent of the people in the United States earned about 5 percent of the money income. Today, after more than 30 years of government efforts to relieve poverty, the bottom 20 percent still earn about 5 percent of money income. More than 35 million Americans lived in poverty in the mid-1960s; more than 35 million U.S. citizens *still* live in poverty, despite the expenditure of hundreds of billions of dollars in aid for the poor. Are U.S. efforts to aid the poor winning the war on poverty? Or are these efforts simply shifting the field of battle?

If we are to answer such questions, we must begin by getting the facts straight. First, even though the absolute number of Americans living in poverty has not diminished appreciably over the past three decades, population growth has brought a slight reduction in the *proportion* of impoverished Americans. As conventionally measured, more than 17 percent of Americans lived in poverty in 1965; today about 15 percent of the population is below the poverty line.

Second, traditional methods of measuring poverty may be misleading, because they focus solely on the *cash incomes* of individuals. In effect, government statisticians compute a "minimum adequate" budget for families of various sizes—the "poverty line"—and then determine how many people have cash incomes below this line. Yet major components of the federal government's antipoverty efforts come in the form of **in-kind transfers** (transfers of goods and services, rather than cash) such as Medicare, Medicaid, subsidized housing, food stamps, school lunches, and so forth. When the dollar value of these in-kind transfers is included in measures of *total* income, the standard of living of persons at lower income levels has improved substantially over the years—relative to the "official numbers," and compared to the rest of society.

There is disagreement over how much of these in-kind transfers should be included in measures of the total income of recipients.[1] Nevertheless, most observers agree that over the last 30 years, the proportion of Americans living below the poverty line has been cut almost in half. Just as important, when in-kind transfers are taken into account, the share of total income going to the poorest 20 percent of the population has more than doubled since the mid-1960s. In short, the number of poor individuals in this country has declined significantly, and those who remain are generally better off than the poor of 30 years ago.

The conclusion that cash income is an inadequate measure of poverty is reinforced if we look at the *consumption* expenditures made at various levels of income. Consumption can differ from measured income for a variety of reasons. In addition to the in-kind transfers just mentioned, consumption spending can exceed measured income when people work in the informal or underground sectors of the economy and do not report all of their earnings. Moreover, people can consume more than they earn if they own assets, such as houses. (According to surveys by the Census Bureau and the Department of Housing and Urban Development, 40 percent of all poor households own their own homes, the overwhelming majority of which are in good condition.) The results of taking these factors into account are striking. According to Professor Daniel Slesnick of the University of Texas, when measured in terms of consumption, the level of inequality in the United States has dropped 23 percent over the last half-century. And although most of this drop occurred between 1958 and 1973, there was no reversal in the 1980s, as is commonly suggested by the data on cash income. Harvard economist Dale Jorgenson is even more forceful in his conclusions, asserting that "The corrected statistics show that the standard of living is rising, inequality is falling, and poverty is disappearing."

Whatever measure of income we use, it is crucial to remember that most Americans exhibit a great deal of **income mobility**—they

---

[1] There are two reasons for this disagreement. First, a given dollar amount of in-kind transfers is generally less valuable than the same dollar amount of cash income, because cash offers the recipient a greater amount of choice in his or her consumption pattern. Second, medical care is an important in-kind transfer to the poor. Inclusion of all Medicaid expenditures for the poor would imply that the sicker the poor got, the richer they would be. Presumably, a correct measure would include only those medical expenses that the poor would have to incur if they were *not* poor, and thus had to pay for the medical care (or medical insurance) out of their own pockets.

have a tendency to move around in the **income distribution** over time. The most important source of income mobility is the "life-cycle" pattern of earnings: new entrants to the work force tend to have lower incomes at first, but typically can look forward to rising incomes as they gain experience on the job. Typically, annual earnings reach a maximum at about age 55. Because peak earnings occur well beyond the **median age** of the population (now about age 33), a "snapshot" of the current distribution of earnings will find most individuals "on the way up" toward a higher position in the income distribution. People who have low earnings now are likely, on average, to have *higher* earnings in the future.

Another major source of income mobility stems from the operation of "lady luck." At any point in time, the income of high-income people is likely to be abnormally high (relative to what they can expect on average) due to recent "good luck," for example, because they just won the Florida lottery, or just received a long-awaited bonus. Conversely, the income of people who currently have low incomes is likely to be abnormally low due to recent "bad luck," for example, because they are laid up after an automobile accident, or recently have become temporarily unemployed. Over time, the effects of lady luck tend to average out across the population. Accordingly, people with high income today will tend to have lower income in the future, while people with low income today will tend to have higher future income; equivalently, many people living below the poverty line are there temporarily rather than permanently.

The impact of the forces that produce income mobility are strikingly revealed in studies examining the incomes of individuals over time. During the 1970s and 1980s, for example, among the people who were in the top 20 percent of income earners at the beginning of the decade, less than *half* were in the top 20 percent by the end of the decade. Similarly, among the people who were in the bottom 20 percent income bracket at the beginning of the decade, almost half had moved out of that bracket by the end of the decade.

Now that we can see that income numbers do not always mean what they seem, let us look at some of the other characteristics of the poor. In the mid-1960s, three groups were most at risk of being poor: blacks, the elderly, and women. The incidence of poverty among the elderly, for example, was more than double that of the rest of the population. Today, although many single elderly people remain poor, the poverty rate among the elderly is *lower* than for the rest of the population. An important reason for this reversal is the introduction of Medicare and the large increase in Social Security benefits that has taken place. In effect, today's retirees are being subsidized out of the payroll taxes levied on today's workers.

While blacks still earn less than whites on average, the income gap between the two races has narrowed markedly. In the early 1960s, black men earned only about 30 percent as much as white men; today this ratio is about 75 percent. The pay earned by black women has risen from 54 percent of white women's pay to better than 97 percent. Despite these improvements, there still remains a sizable income gap between blacks and whites in the United States. Moreover, the corporate bureaucracy remains predominately white, and many blacks feel that race still plays a role in evaluations of their job performance. As one black senior manager puts it, "If you're a black boss, you're probably second-guessed more."

The economic position of women also has improved markedly during the last 30 years. Importantly, this has been due to a massive increase in the number of women entering the labor force; labor force participation by women has risen more than 50 percent since the mid-1960s. Although crude measures of wages show only a modest increase in women's pay relative to men's pay—with women now earning just over 75 percent of what men receive—many studies suggest that this apparent disparity is due largely to occupational choices made by women. Many females continue to choose career paths that offer the greatest freedom in mixing family and work responsibilities. In jobs most nearly identical to those held by men, women's wages have risen relative to men's wages over the last 30 years; women are gradually moving into positions that require a stronger commitment to long-term labor-force attachment—and are being paid correspondingly higher wages as a result. Despite this, many women feel that it is far too often they, rather than their male counterparts, who have to make the toughest choices between family and work responsibilities.

The modest reduction in poverty over the past 30 years has occurred chiefly because of the hard work and sheer determination of the individuals who have made the journey up the ladder of economic progress. Nevertheless, the upward migration of the poor of the 1960s has been accompanied by substantial costs for other members of society—including *today's* poor.

All government programs that transfer wealth among individuals affect people's decisions about how much and what type of work to do. Financing the programs requires higher taxes than would otherwise be the case. This reduces people's take-home pay, inducing some to work less, others to work less hard, and still others to refrain from working at all. The reduction in work effort means lower total income for society as a whole. The higher taxation also induces some people to take measures to avoid or evade those taxes. They concoct tax shelter schemes, whose purpose is not productive activity, but simply tax avoidance, or they refrain from socially productive saving and investment because high tax rates lower their own private return from such activity. Again, the result is lower wealth for society as a whole. Finally, the cash and in-kind benefits offered by government transfer programs induce counter-productive behavior on the part of recipients. Some choose leisure rather than work, because the pay is almost as good; fathers leave their families to enable the latter to qualify for federal aid; and some people migrate to states offering higher welfare benefits. In each case, the incentives of the programs induce people to undertake actions that are in their own best interests, but which reduce the total income available to society as a whole.

Estimating the magnitude of the "efficiency losses"—the economic cost to society—of our income-transfer programs is no easy task, and one sure to provoke controversy. Undaunted, economists have tried, and concluded that the losses are at least 35 percent of the amount taken from upper income people. Considering that we now spend over $500 billion per year on income transfer programs, the magnitude of the probable loss is truly staggering. Such figures illustrate that, like most things in life, the reduction of poverty is not free. Ironically, one of the most significant costs of the government's effort to alleviate poverty is measurable not in dollars and cents, but in its impact on the structure of U.S. families, particularly minority families.

Among the 35 million or so people living below the poverty line in the United States today, two groups predominate: youths (particularly minority youths) and single-parent families. Regardless of their education, young people today earn less relative to older workers (ages 35–54) than they did 25 years ago. Among men ages 16–24 without a high school diploma, for example, the deterioration in relative earnings exceeds 10 percent. Among all youths, unemployment has increased drastically; the youth unemployment rate during the 1980s and 1990s has been double the level of the 1960s.

The deteriorating economic status of minority youngsters is exceeded only by that of families headed by women. Compared to two-parent families, the per capita income of white, mother-only families has fallen more than 10 percent since the 1960s; among blacks, the deterioration is 20 percent. Moreover, the number of these families has increased markedly. In the mid-1960s, only about 10 percent of all families were headed by a single mother; today the figure exceeds 20 percent. More than *half* of all black families are now headed by women.

The enormous growth in numbers and dire financial conditions of female-headed households is reflected in the rising poverty rate of children. Twenty-five years ago the poverty rate among children was not much above that of the rest of the population. Today, children are 50 percent more likely to live in poverty than the rest of the population. Indeed, almost half of today's poor are children—mostly children in families headed by women. As these figures suggest, the modest reduction in poverty occurring over the past 30 years has been accompanied by a major alteration in the identities of the poor. The upward mobility of the poor of the 1960s—black males, women, and the elderly—has been accompanied by the downward mobility of many of today's poor. Indeed, one of the most ironic and tragic costs of the government's effort to alleviate poverty has been its impact on the structure of U.S. families, particularly minority families.

In general, poverty programs are means-tested, that is, if a person's or a family's income is judged by the government to be too high, eligibility for benefits is reduced or eliminated. For most families, the father is—or ordinarily would be—the primary source of income. If the family's income is above but close to the means-test level, there often is a financial incentive for the father to leave the family unit, so that his income is excluded when the family's eligibility is determined. And, because eligibility is normally reviewed on a frequent basis, the departure is often permanent, except perhaps for occasional covert visits. Thus the existence of welfare programs, such as Aid to Families with Dependent Children (AFDC), actually encourages the breakup of the family unit: either marriage never takes place, or the marriage is dissolved by separation or divorce, so that eligibility for federal benefits may be retained or achieved.

Many observers thus argue that the financial incentives of welfare are responsible for the erosion of the two-parent family among blacks. Thirty years ago, for example, black women and white women were quite similar in marital status: about two-thirds of each group were married. Today, although more than 60 percent of white women are married, only 40 percent of black women are married. Partly because of this decline in marriage among blacks, the incidence of illegitimate births among blacks is at record-high levels: more than 60 percent of all black children are born out of wedlock, a rate triple that observed among whites. This striking pattern may be encouraged by the very structure of AFDC payments. Because each additional child brings higher AFDC payments for the family, the welfare system provides a modest financial inducement for AFDC recipients to have more children. In short, many observers now believe that the government's efforts to relieve poverty have both altered the composition of the poor population and encouraged more poverty. Because the structure of the system discourages two-parent families among low-income individuals, and encourages the birth of additional children, we now have a population of the poor that is dominated by single-parent heads of households and children.

The recognition that past and current government programs have actually helped create and shape the current population of the poor raises a troubling question: What changes in policy are appropriate in dealing with poverty? Over the past 15 years, several attempts have been made to answer this question, but the long-term implications of the new policies are far from clear.

In 1981, the largely ineffective federal system of job training developed in the 1970s was abolished and replaced by the Job Training Partnership Act (JTPA). Under this program, instead of day-to-day decisions about the use of funds being made in Washington, D.C., monies have been handed out to state and local governments to use as they see fit, as long as those uses are consistent with the overall training objectives of JTPA. Job placement rates for JTPA graduates appear to be higher than in any previous federal job training program, but these results may be due largely to the fact that the program has been more selective in picking its trainees. Only time—and careful scrutiny—will tell.

The government also has begun to alter its approach to providing housing assistance for the poor. For many years, the standard strategy had focused chiefly on the construction of huge, high-density apartment complexes in deteriorating inner cities. Despite their high cost (about $90,000 per dwelling unit in 1996 dollars), the location and design of these public housing projects often turned them into "instant slums"—breeding grounds for crime and drugs. The construction of such projects has been eliminated for the most part; today the emphasis is on providing housing subsidies for the poor, in the form of housing **vouchers**, and letting *them* choose where to live.

On a more limited scale, there has been experimentation with reforming the welfare system. Principal among the approaches has been the limited introduction of workfare, in which some AFDC recipients are required to work in return for a portion of their welfare payments. To date, there is simply too little evidence on the workfare approach to assess its long-term implications.

In a variety of dimensions, the focus of the federal government in recent years has been to eliminate programs that simply "throw money" at the problems of the poor, and to reduce the intrusiveness of the federal bureaucracy in decision making. At the governmental level, this has meant increased reliance on activity and decision making by state and local authorities. At the individual level, it has meant added freedom—and responsibility—for the poor themselves. As yet, it is unclear whether the new focus will markedly reduce poverty or perhaps simply create a new bottom tier of individuals unable to cope with the current rules of the game.

DISCUSSION QUESTIONS

1. Why do most modern societies try to reduce poverty? Why don't they do so by simply passing a law that requires that everybody have the same income?

2. How do the "rules of the game" help determine who will be poor and who will not?

3. Which of the following possible in-kind transfers do you think raises the "true" incomes of recipients the most: (1) free golf lessons; (2) free transportation on public buses; or (3) free food?

4. Consider three alternative ways of helping poor people get better housing: (1) government subsidized housing that costs $3000 per year; (2) a housing voucher worth $3000 per year toward rent on an apartment or a house; or (3) $3000 per year in cash. Which would you prefer if you were poor? On what grounds might you make your decision?

23

Where There's Smoking, There's Fire

Thirty-five years ago smoking existed everywhere; indeed, it was something of a status symbol to smoke. Television ads and movies showed the heroes and heroines dangling cigarettes from their mouths. Since then, the image of the smoker has changed dramatically. Smokers are now condemned by many as self-indulgent, self-destructive polluters who are inconsiderate of the effect their smoke has on others nearby. Recent opinion polls show that nearly 90 percent of nonsmokers think that smokers should refrain from smoking when others are present. Yet polls show also that, while smokers may be self-indulgent and self-destructive, they are not all inconsiderate of others: More than 60 percent of smokers agree with the nonsmokers that smokers should not inflict their smoke on third parties.

The beginning of this dramatic change in attitude toward smoking dates from the 1964 Surgeon General's report, which made it clear that smoking is harmful to health. As the link between lung cancer and smoking became established more firmly, increasingly stern labels were required on cigarette packages to warn consumers of the health hazards caused by smoking.

In recent years, the focus has been broadened to include the adverse health effects of smoking on "passive smokers," nonsmokers who are continually exposed to smoke-filled air either at home or in the workplace. One study estimated that 5000 Americans die every year as a result of secondhand smoke, and a recent Japanese report concluded that wives of heavy smokers had an 80 percent higher risk of developing lung cancer than women married to nonsmokers. Heart disease has also been connected to passive smoking. The exact degree to which smoking physically harms non-smokers, though, is still under debate; vehement proponents of the rights of smokers can cite several scientific studies that have been unable to establish a relationship between "passive" smoking and significant harmful health effects. But there is no doubt that smoking can be irritating and obnoxious for the nonsmoker and that, whether they want to or not, nonsmokers are forced to breathe the polluted air created by smokers in numerous situations.

Smoking is a classic case of a **negative externality**, one for which it would be appropriate for the smoker to compensate the nonsmoker for the discomfort felt, according to the efficiency standards of the economist. In the absence of compensation, the correct policy might be to impose rules and regulations that prevent the smoker from being able to irritate the nonsmoker. Why doesn't the federal government simply ban smoking? Ultimately, the issue becomes one of political economy, in which the interests of competing groups are balanced—often with peculiar results. On the one hand, the Surgeon General's reports have resulted in a heavily subsidized publicity campaign to prevent smoking. On the other hand, the 130,000 or so growers of tobacco in the United States profit from laws that restrict tobacco acreage and provide a prohibitive tax of 75 percent on all tobacco grown on unlicensed land. The result is large monopoly returns to those growers fortunate enough to have been in on the beginning of this subsidy (which started some six decades ago).

There's still more to the hand of government. The low **elasticity of demand** for tobacco makes it an excellent source of tax revenue. Indeed, federal tax receipts from the sale of cigarettes now run about $5 billion per year, and this does not include receipts from import duties on tobacco and tobacco products. Clearly, some parts of the federal government feel they have a great deal to gain from the continued use of tobacco, as does the subsidized farmer in the south, and the 46 million Americans who call themselves smokers, who spend over $40 billion a year for tobacco products.

There is little doubt that if tobacco were discovered for the first time today it would be put in the same class as cocaine, heroin, and other dangerous drugs, and be considered something that should be outlawed by society. But smoking became a national craze in an era when it was viewed as prestigious. Also, smokers are voters, as are tobacco growers and the growing legions of antismokers. As a result, it is not surprising that the politics of smoking should lead to contradictory roles of government—where the left hand works to prohibit smoking and the right hand subsidizes tobacco farmers.

State and local governments provide an interesting illustration of the forces of political economy behind the seemingly contradictory behavior of the federal government. To date, 46 states and more than 400 local governments have enacted rules restricting smoking. Not surprisingly, these restrictions are more prevalent where tobacco is an unimportant part of the local economy. In 1975 Minnesota became the first state to pass a comprehensive clean indoor-air act. In contrast, Virginia, where tobacco is a $3-billion-a-year industry, actually passed legislation outlawing discrimination against smokers. New York City, whose then-mayor had not smoked since 1952, not only passed stiff legislation restricting smoking in public, but also hired 70 smoke police to enforce the rules. Meanwhile, most cities and counties in tobacco states such as Kentucky, Virginia, and the Carolinas have steadfastly refused to seriously limit where smokers may light up.

A look across our northern border also helps to illustrate the forces of political economy, and demonstrates that the law of demand applies even to an addictive drug like nicotine. Although tobacco is grown and cigarettes are produced in Canada (predominantly in southern Ontario), these industries play a smaller role in the Canadian economy than in the U.S. economy, suggesting that their political clout should be smaller in Canada. Moreover, the health care system in Canada is run by the government, so that a much larger proportion of the health care costs associated with smoking are borne by the taxpayers rather than by the individuals who are doing the smoking. Thus, beginning about 15 years ago, the Canadian federal and provincial governments launched an all-out assault on smoking. Virtually all cigarette advertising has been banned in Canada, and health warnings are now required to take up more than 20 percent of the front and back of all cigarette packs sold in Canada. The spearhead of the assault, however, has been the attack on smokers' pocketbooks. Increases in Canadian federal and provincial cigarette taxes pushed inflation-adjusted cigarette prices up 152 percent from 1982 to 1992. And although cigarette bootlegging forced the Canadians to cut taxes in 1994, the average retail price per pack of cigarettes in Canada is still about $4.70.

The tax-induced rise in the price of cigarettes in Canada has had just the effect predicted by the law of demand: smoking has declined sharply. Studies of the demand for cigarettes generally estimate that the elasticity of demand for cigarettes is around –0.4, which means that each 10 percent rise in their inflation-adjusted price induces a 4 percent drop in consumption. And according to David Sweanor of Canada's Non-smokers' Rights Association, "That's just about what we've been finding." Overall, per capita adult smoking in Canada has plunged 43 percent, and smoking among teenagers has dropped 61 percent.

In the United States, only a few states, such as California, Minnesota, and Wisconsin, have been quite so vigorous in using tax policy to discourage smoking. Nevertheless, the private sector is becoming more active in clearing the haze, both on and off the job.

Within the business community, more than half of all firms have restrictions on smoking at work. Some ban smoking on the job altogether, and roughly 6 percent of all firms refuse to hire smokers. At some firms, smoking *off* the job is grounds for dismissal. Importantly, firms are cracking down on smokers because of the growing evidence that smoking reduces productivity and also raises company health insurance costs. Their policies also seem to be influenced, however, by the habits of top management: When the boss smokes, employee smoking is more likely to be tolerated. This fact alone suggests that additional workplace smoking restrictions are likely in the future. Over the past decade or so, white-collar workers have been much more diligent in curbing their smoking appetites than have blue-collar workers. It is estimated today that smoking among white-collar workers is only *half* as prevalent as among blue-collar workers.[1] As the smoke-free yuppies of the 1980s become the bosses of the 1990s and beyond, cleaner air on the job is likely to follow.

[1] This pattern is hardly surprising. White-collar workers are, on average, better educated and thus more likely to be aware of the full range of hazards associated with smoking. They also tend to earn higher incomes; a 10 percent loss in output (and thus income) from smoking for a person capable when healthy of earning $100,000 a year is clearly more expensive than a 10 percent loss in output for a person who is worth, say, $20,000 a year at peak performance.

As the smoke clears, there is a certain irony in the spreading restrictions against lighting up. For many years in this country, chewers of tobacco outnumbered smokers. Early in this century social reformers, concerned about the spread of tuberculosis, launched a campaign to prohibit public spitting—an activity developed into an art form by tobacco chewers. Faced with a compelling community health problem, town after town imposed a ban on spitting. Unwilling to fight, Americans seeking a nicotine jolt thus made a large-scale switch to the "safer" alternative—cigarettes. So much for progress.

DISCUSSION QUESTIONS

1. How would you compare the problem of air pollution created by smokers to that of pollution created by industrial plants?

2. According to the law of demand, an increase in the price of cigarettes will induce people to smoke less. Since governments have the power to tax, they have the power to raise the price of cigarettes. Given this fact, why do governments often choose to regulate smoking (e.g., prohibiting it in certain places) rather than simply taxing it?

3. There is growing evidence that foods high in saturated fats are harmful to people's health. Why do we have warning labels on cigarette packs but don't have warning labels on french fries and potato chips?

4. If cigarettes are harmful to those who smoke them and to people exposed to others' smoke, why doesn't the government prohibit cigarette smoking completely, just as it prohibits the smoking of crack (cocaine)?

Part Six

Externalities and the Environment

INTRODUCTION

We saw in Part Three that monopoly and monopsony produce outcomes that differ significantly from the competitive outcome, and so yield gains from trade that fall short of the competitive ideal. In Part Six we see that when externalities are present—that is, when there are discrepancies between the private costs of action and the social costs of action—the competitive outcome differs from the competitive ideal. Typically, the problem in the case of externalities is said to be "market failure," but the diagnosis might just as well be termed "government failure." For markets to work efficiently, property rights to scarce goods must be well-defined, cheaply enforceable, and fully transferable, and it is generally the government that is believed to have a comparative advantage in ensuring that these conditions are satisfied. If the government fails to define, enforce, or make transferable property rights, the market will generally fail to produce socially efficient outcomes, and it becomes a moot point as to who is at fault. The real point is this: What might be done to improve things?

As population and per capita income both rise, consumption, rises faster than either, for it responds to the combined impetus of both. With consumption comes the residue of consumption, also known as plain old garbage. Many of us have heard of landfills being closed because of fears of groundwater contamination, or of homeless garbage scows wandering the high seas in search of a place to off-load; all of us have been bombarded with public service messages to recycle everything from aluminum cans to old newspapers. The United States, it seems, is becoming the garbage capital of the world. This is no doubt true, but it is also true that the United States is the professional football capital of the world—and yet pro football teams seem to have no problem finding cities across the country willing to welcome them with open arms. What is different about garbage? You are probably inclined to answer that football is enjoyable and garbage is not. True enough, but this is not why garbage sometimes piles up faster than anyone seems willing to dispose of it. Garbage becomes a problem only if it is not priced properly; that is, if the consumers and businesses that produce it are not charged enough for its removal, and the landfills where it is deposited are not paid enough for its disposal. The message of Chapter 24, "The Trashman Cometh," is that garbage really is not different from the things we consume in the course of producing it. As long as the trashman is paid, he will cometh, and as long as we have to pay for his services, his burden will be bearable. We will still have garbage, but we will not have a garbage problem.

We noted earlier that the property rights to a scarce good or resource must be clearly defined, fully enforced, and readily transferable if that resource is to be used efficiently—that is, in the manner that yields the greatest net benefits. This is true whether the resource in question is space in a landfill, water in a stream, or, as we see in Chapter 25, "Bye, Bye, Bison," members of an animal species. If these conditions are satisfied, the resource will be used in the manner that benefits both its owner and society the most. If these conditions are not satisfied—as they were not for American bison on the hoof or passenger pigeons on the wing—the resource generally will not be used in the most efficient manner. And in the case of animal species that are competing with human beings, this sometimes means extinction. What should be done when a species becomes endangered? If our desire is to produce the greatest net benefit to humanity, the answer in general is not to protect the species at any possible cost, for this would be equivalent to assigning an infinite value to the species. Instead, the proper course of action is to devise rules that induce people to act as though the members of the species were private property. If such rules can be developed, we shall not have to worry about spotted owls or African elephants becoming extinct any more than we currently worry about parakeets or cocker spaniels becoming extinct.

In Chapter 26, "Smog Merchants," property rights are again the focus of the discussion as we look at air pollution. We ordinarily think of the air around us as being something that we all "own." The practical consequence of this is that we act as though the air is owned by none of us—for no one can exclude anyone else from using "our" air. As a result, we overuse the air in the sense that air pollution becomes a problem. This chapter shows that it is possible to define and enforce property rights to air, which the owners can then use as they see fit—which includes selling the rights to others. Once this is done, the users of clean air have the incentive to use it just as efficiently as they do all of the other resources (such as land, labor, and capital) utilized in the production process.

Air—or more generally, the atmosphere as a whole—reappears as the topic of Chapter 27, "Greenhouse Economics." There is a growing body of evidence that human action is responsible for growing concentrations of so-called "greenhouse gases" in the earth's atmosphere, and that left unchecked this growth may produce costly increases in the average temperature of our planet. Given the nature of the problem—a **negative externality**—private action taken on the individual level will not yield the optimal outcome for society. Thus the potential gains from government action, in the form of environmental regulations or taxation, are substantial. The key word here is potential, for government action, no matter how well-intentioned, does not automatically yield benefits that exceed the costs. As we seek solutions to the potential problems associated with greenhouse gases, we must be sure that the consequences of premature action are not worse than those of first examining the problem further. If we forget this message, greenhouse economics may turn into bad economics—and worse policy.

24

The Trashman Cometh

Is garbage really different? To answer this question, let us consider a simple hypothetical situation. Suppose a city agreed to provide its residents with all of the food they wished to consume, prepared in the manner they specified, and delivered to their homes for a flat, monthly fee that was independent of what or how much they ate. What are the likely consequences of this city food delivery service? Most likely, people in the city would begin to eat more, because the size of their food bill would be independent of the amount they ate. They would also be more likely to consume lobster and filet mignon rather than fish sticks and hamburger because, once again, the cost to them would be independent of their menu selections. Soon the city's food budget would be astronomical, and either the monthly fee or taxes would have to be increased. People from other communities might even begin moving (or at least making extended visits) to the city, just to partake of this wonderful service. Within short order the city would face a "food crisis" as it sought to cope with providing a rapidly growing amount of food from a city budget that could no longer handle the financial burden.

If this story sounds silly to you, just change "food delivery" to "garbage pick-up"; what we have just described is the way most cities in the country have operated their municipal garbage collection services. The result during the past decade was the appearance of a "garbage crisis"—with overflowing landfills, homeless garbage scows, and drinking-water wells polluted with the run-off from trash heaps. This seeming crisis—to the extent it existed—was fundamentally no different from the "food crisis" described above. The problem was not that (1) almost nobody wants garbage, nor that (2) garbage has adverse environmental effects, nor even that (3) we had too much garbage. The *problem* lay in that (1) we ordinarily do not put prices on garbage in the way we put prices on the goods that generate the garbage, and (2) a strange assortment of bedfellows used a few smelly facts to make things seem worse than they were.

First things first. America is producing garbage at a record rate: In 1995 we generated about 200 million tons of household and commercial solid waste that either had to be burned or buried. (That works out to almost 1500 pounds *per person*.) More than one-third of this was paper, while yard waste (such as grass trimmings) accounted for another 20 percent. Plastics amounted to about 20 percent of the volume of material that had to be disposed of, but because plastic is relatively light, it comprised only about 8 percent of the weight. Had there been no recycling, probably we would have had to dispose of another 25 to 30 million tons of assorted trash.

Landfills are the final resting place for most of our garbage, although incineration is also widely used in some areas, particularly in the Northeast, where land values are high. Over the last decade, both methods began falling out of favor with people who lived near these facilities (or might eventually), as NIMBY (not-in-my-backyard) attitudes spread across the land. Federal, state, and local regulations made it increasingly difficult to establish new waste disposal facilities, or even to keep old ones operating. The cost to open a modern 100-acre landfill rose to an estimated $65 million or more, and the permit process needed to open a new disposal facility soared to 7 years in some states. Meanwhile, environmental concerns forced the closure of many landfills throughout the country, and prevented others from ever beginning operations. By 1992, all but five states were exporting at least some of their garbage to other states. Today, most of the garbage from some densely populated states in the Northeast ends up in other people's backyards: New Jersey ships garbage to 10 other states, while New York keeps landfill operators busy in 13 different states. Across the country, Americans have begun to wonder where all of the garbage is going to go.

Although the failure of America's cities to price garbage appropriately led to an inefficient amount of the stuff, much of the appearance of a garbage crisis has been misleading. Rubbish first hit the headlines in 1987 when a garbage barge named the *Mobro*, headed south with New York City trash, couldn't find a home for its load. As it turns out, the barge operator hadn't nailed down a satisfactory disposal contract before he sailed; when he tried to conduct negotiations over the radio while underway, operators of likely landfills (mistakenly) suspected he might be carrying toxic waste rather than routine trash. When adverse publicity forced the barge back to New York with its load, many people thought it was a lack of landfill space, rather than poor planning by the barge operator, that was the cause. This notion was reinforced by an odd combination of environmental groups, waste management firms, and the Environmental Protection Agency (EPA).

The Environmental Defense Fund wanted to start a major campaign to push recycling, and the *Mobro* gave things the push it needed. As one official for the organization noted, "An advertising firm couldn't have designed a better vehicle than a garbage barge." Meanwhile, a number of farsighted waste management companies had begun loading up on landfill space, taking advantage of new technologies that increased the efficient minimum size of a disposal facility. Looking to get firm contracts for filling this space, the trade group for the disposal industry started pushing the notion that America was running out of dump space. State and local officials who relied on the group's data quickly bought into the new landfills, paying premium prices to do so. The EPA, meanwhile, was studying the garbage problem, but without accounting for the fact that its own regulations were causing the efficient scale of landfills to double and even quadruple in size. Thus, the EPA merely counted landfills around the country and reported that they were shrinking in number. This was true enough, but what the EPA failed to report was that because landfills were getting bigger much faster than they were closing down, total disposal capacity was *growing* rapidly, not shrinking.

For a while, it seemed that recycling was going to take care of what appeared to be a growing trash problem. In 1987, for example, old newspapers were selling for as much as $60 per ton, and many municipalities felt that the answer to their financial woes and garbage troubles was at hand. Yet as more communities began putting mandatory recycling laws into effect, the prices of recycled trash began to plummet. Over the next 5 years, 3500 communities in more than half the states had some form of mandatory curbside recycling; the resulting increase in the supply of used newsprint meant that by 1992, communities were having to *pay* to have the stuff carted away—a situation that continues today. For glass and plastics, the story is so far much the same: The market value of the used materials is below the cost of collecting and sorting it. About a dozen states have acted to increase the demand for old newsprint by requiring locally published newspapers to utilize a minimum content of recycled newsprint. Even so, many experts believe that no more than 60 to 70 percent of all newsprint can be recycled, and we are already recycling 44 percent of it, up from 33 percent in 1988.

Just as significantly, recycling raises significant issues that were often ignored during the early rush to embrace the concept. For example, the production of 100 tons of de-inked fiber from old newsprint produces about 40 tons of sludge that must be disposed of somehow. Although the total volume of material is reduced, the concentrated form of what is left can make it more costly to dispose of properly. Similarly, recycling paper is unlikely to save trees, for most virgin newsprint is made from trees planted expressly for that purpose and harvested as a crop: If recycling increases, many of these trees simply will not be planted. In a study done for Resources for the Future, A. Clark Wiseman concluded, "The likely effect of [newsprint recycling] appears to be smaller, rather than larger, forest inventory." Moreover, most virgin newsprint is made in Canada, using clean hydroelectric power. Makers of newsprint in the United States (the primary customers for the recycled stuff) often use higher-polluting energy such as coal. Thus, one potential side effect of recycling is the switch from hydroelectric power to fossil fuels.

Some have argued that we should simply ban certain products. For example, styrofoam cups have gotten a bad name because they take up more space in landfills than do paper hot-drink cups, and because the styrofoam remains in the landfill forever. Yet according to a widely-cited study by Martin B. Hockman of the University of Victoria, the manufacture of a paper cup consumes 36 times as much electricity and generates 580 times as much waste water as does the manufacture of a styrofoam cup. Moreover, as paper degrades underground, it releases methane, a "greenhouse gas" that contributes to warming the atmosphere. In a similar vein, consider disposable diapers, which have been trashed by their opponents because a week's worth generates 22.2

pounds of post-use waste, while a week's worth of reusable diapers generates only 0.24 pounds. Because disposable diapers already amount to 2 percent of the nation's solid waste, the edge clearly seems to go to reusable cloth diapers. Yet the use of reusable rather than disposable diapers consumes more than three times as many Btus (British thermal units) of energy and generates ten times as much water pollution. It would seem that the trade-offs that are present when we talk about "goods" are just as prevalent when we discuss "bads" such as garbage.

It also appears that more government regulation of the garbage business is likely to make things worse rather than better, as may be illustrated by the tale of two states: New Jersey and Pennsylvania. A number of years ago, to stop what was described as price-gouging by organized crime, New Jersey decided to regulate waste hauling and disposal as a public utility. Once the politicians got involved in the trash business, however, politics very nearly destroyed the business of trash. According to Paul Kleindorfer of the University of Pennsylvania, political opposition to passing garbage disposal costs along to consumers effectively ended investment in landfills. In 1972 there were 331 landfills operating in New Jersey; by 1988 the number had fallen to 13, because the state-regulated fees payable to landfill operators simply didn't cover the rising costs of operation. Half of New Jersey's municipal solid waste is now exported to neighboring Pennsylvania.

Pennsylvania's situation provides a sharp contrast. The state does not regulate the deals that communities make with landfill and incinerator operators; the market takes care of matters instead. For example, despite the state's hands-off policy, "tipping fees" (the charges for disposing of garbage in landfills) are below the national average in Pennsylvania, effectively limited by competition between disposal facilities. The market seems to be providing the right incentives; in one recent year, there were 31 pending applications to open landfills in Pennsylvania, but only 2 in New Jersey, despite the fact that New Jersey residents are paying the highest disposal rates in the country to ship garbage as far away as Michigan, Illinois, Missouri, and Alabama.

Ultimately, there are two issues that must be solved when it comes to trash. First, what do we do with it once we have it? Second, how do we reduce the amount of it that we have? As hinted at by the Pennsylvania story, and illustrated further by developments elsewhere in the country, the market mechanism can answer both questions. The fact of the matter is that in many areas of the country, population densities are high and land is expensive. As a result, a large amount of trash is produced and it is expensive to dispose of locally. In contrast, there are some areas of the country where there are relatively few people around to produce garbage, where land for disposal facilities is cheap, and where wide open spaces minimize the potential air pollution hazards associated with incinerators. The sensible thing to do, it would seem, is to have the states that produce most of the trash ship it to states where it can be most efficiently disposed of—for a price, of course. This is already being done to an extent, but residents of potential recipient states are (not surprisingly) concerned, lest they end up being the garbage capitals of the nation. Yet Wisconsin, which imports garbage from as far away as New Jersey, is demonstrating that it is possible to get rid of the trash without trashing the neighborhood. Landfill operators in Wisconsin are now required to send water table monitoring reports to neighbors, and to maintain the landfills for 40 years after closure. Operators also have guaranteed the value of neighboring homes to gain the permission of nearby residents, and in some cases even have purchased homes to quiet neighbors' objections. These features all add to the cost of operating landfills, but as long as prospective customers are willing to pay the price and neighboring residents are satisfied with their protections—and so far these conditions appear to be satisfied—then it would seem tough to argue with the outcome.

Some might still argue that it does not seem right for one community to be able to dump its trash elsewhere. Yet the flip side is this: Is it right to *prevent* communities from accepting the trash, if that is what they want? Consider Gillam County, Oregon (pop. 1800), which wanted Seattle's garbage so badly it fought Oregon state legislators' attempts to tax out-of-state trash coming into Oregon. Seattle's decision to use the Gillam County landfill will generate $1 million per year for the little community—some 25 percent of its annual budget, and enough to finance the operations of the county's largest school.

Faced with the prospect of paying to dispose of its garbage, Seattle quickly had to confront the problem of reducing the amount of trash its residents were generating. Its solution was to charge householders according to the amount they put out. Seattle thus began charging $13.50 per month for weekly pickup of one can, plus $9 for each additional can. Yard waste that has been separated for composting costs $2 per month, while paper, glass, and metal separated for recycling are hauled away at no charge. In the first year that per-can charges were imposed, the total tonnage that had to be buried fell by 22 percent. Voluntary recycling rose from 24 percent of waste to 36 percent—a rate almost triple the national average. By 1994, the "Seattle Stomp" (used to fit more trash into a can) had become a regular source of exercise, and the city was having trouble exporting *enough* garbage to fulfill its contract with Gillam County.

The message slowly beginning to emerge across the country then, is that garbage really is not different from the things we consume in the course of producing it. As long as the trashman is paid, he will cometh, and as long as we must pay for his services, his burden will be bearable.

DISCUSSION QUESTIONS

1. How do deposits on bottles and cans affect the incentives of individuals to recycle these products?

2. Why do many communities *mandate* recycling? Is it possible to induce people to recycle more without requiring that all residents recycle?

3. How do hefty per-can garbage pickup fees influence the decisions people make about what goods they will *consume*?

4. A community planning on charging a fee for trash pickup might structure the fee in any of several ways. It might, for example, charge (1) a fixed amount per can; (2) an amount per pound of garbage; or (3) a flat fee per month, without regard to amount of garbage. How would each of these affect the amount and type of garbage produced? Which system would lead to an increase in the use of trash compactors? Which would lead to the most garbage?

25

Bye, Bye, Bison

The destruction of animal species by humans is nothing new. For example, the arrival of human beings in North America about 12,000 years ago is tied to the extinction of most of the megafauna (very large animals) which then existed. The famous LaBrea Tarpits of Southern California yielded the remains of 24 mammals and 22 birds that no longer exist. Among these are the saber-toothed tiger, the giant llama, the 20-foot ground sloth, and a bison that stood 7 feet at the hump and had 6-foot-wide horns.

While many experts believe that human hunting was directly responsible for the destruction of these species, and that a combination of hunting and habitat destruction by humans have led to the extinction of many other species, the link is not always as clear as it might seem at first glance. For example, it is estimated that only about 0.02 percent (1 in 5000) of all species that have ever existed are currently extant. Most of these (including the dinosaurs) disappeared long before humans ever made an appearance. The simple fact is that all species compete for the limited resources available, and most species eventually end up competed out of existence, with or without the help of *Homo sapiens*. Just as important is that basic economic principles can help explain why various species are more or less prone to meet their demise at the hands of humans, and what humans might do if they want to delay the extinction of any particular species.[1]

Let's begin with the passenger pigeon, which provides the most famous example of the role of human beings in the extinction of a species. At one time these birds were the most numerous species of birds in North America and perhaps in the world. They nested and

---

[1] We say "delay" rather than "prevent" extinction because there is no evidence to date that any species—*Homo sapiens* included—has any claim on immortality.

migrated together in huge flocks, and probably numbered in the billions. When flocks passed overhead, the sky would be dark with pigeons for days at a time. The famous naturalist John James Audubon measured one roost at 40 miles long and 3 miles wide, with birds stacked from treetop down to nearly ground level. While the Native Americans had long hunted these birds, the demise of the passenger pigeon is usually tied to the arrival of the white man and the demand for pigeons as a source of food and sport. The birds were shot and netted in vast numbers; by the end of the nineteenth century, an animal species that had been looked on as almost indestructible because of its enormous numbers had almost completely disappeared. The last known passenger pigeon died in the Cincinnati Zoo in 1914.

The American bison only narrowly escaped the same fate. The vast herds that roamed the plains were an easy target for hunters; with the advent of the railroad and the need to feed railroad crews as the transcontinental railroads were built, hunters such as Buffalo Bill Cody killed bison by the thousands. As the demand for the fur of the bison increased, it became the target for more hunting. Like the passenger pigeon, the bison had appeared to be indestructible because of its huge numbers, but the species was soon on the way to becoming extinct. Despite the outcries of the Native Americans who found their major food source being decimated, it was not until late in the nineteenth century that any efforts were made to protect the bison.[2]

These two episodes, particularly that of the bison, are generally viewed as classic examples of humankind's inhumanity to our fellow species, as well as to our fellow humans, for many Indian tribes were ultimately devastated by the near demise of the bison. A closer look reveals more than simply wasteful slaughter; it discloses exactly why events progressed as they did, and how we can learn from them to improve modern efforts to protect species threatened by human neighbors.

Native Americans had hunted the bison for many years before the arrival of white men, and are generally portrayed as both care-

[2] For the bison's cousin, the eastern buffalo—which stood 7 feet tall at the shoulder, was 12 feet long, and weighed more than a ton—the efforts came too late. The last known members of the species, a cow and her calf, were killed in 1825 in the Allegheny Mountains.

fully husbanding their prey and generously sharing the meat among tribal members. Yet the braves who rode their horses into the thundering herds marked their arrows so it was clear who had killed the bison. The marked arrows gave the shooter rights to the best parts of the animal. Tribal members who specialized in butchering the kill also received a share as payment for processing the meat. Indeed, the native American hunting parties were organized remarkably like the parties of the white men who followed: *Once they were killed,* the ownership of the bison was clearly defined, fully enforced, and readily transferable. Moreover, the rewards were distributed in accord with the contribution that each had made to the overall success of the hunt.

Matters were different when it came to the ownership rights to living bison herds. Native Americans, like the whites who came later, had no economically practical way to fence in the herds. The bison could (and did) migrate freely from one tribe's territory into the territory of other tribes. If the members of one tribe economized on their kill, their conservation efforts would chiefly provide more meat for another tribe, who might well be their mortal enemies. This fact induced Native Americans to "exploit" the bison, so that the herds disappeared from some traditional territories on the Great Plains by 1840—before Buffalo Bill was even born.

Two factors made the efforts of the white man—the railroad hunters—more destructive, hastening the disappearance of the bison herds. First, the white population (and thus the demand for the meat and hides) was much larger than the Native American population. Second, white men used firearms on the bison—a technological revolution that increased the killing capacity of a given hunter by a factor of 20 or more, compared to the bow and arrow. Nevertheless, the fundamental problem was the same for the white man and Native American alike: The property rights to live bison could not be cheaply established and enforced. To "own" a bison one had to kill it, and so too many bison were killed.

In economics, the property rights to a scarce good or resource must be clearly defined, fully enforced, and readily transferable if

---

[3] See Ronald Coase, "The Problem of Social Cost," *Journal of Law & Economics,* October 1960, pp. 1–44. This does not mean that all species will be permanently protected from extinction, for reasons that are suggested in Chapter 2, "Flying the Friendly Skies?" It does mean that extinction will be permitted to occur only if the benefits of doing so exceed the costs.

that resource is to be used efficiently—that is, in the manner that yields the greatest net benefits. This is true whether the resource in question is the American bison, the water in a stream, or a pepperoni pizza. If these conditions are satisfied, the resource will be used in the manner that benefits both its owner and society in the greatest manner possible.[3] If they are not satisfied—as they were not for bison on the hoof or passenger pigeons on the wing—the resource generally will not be used in the most efficient manner. In the case of animal species that are competing with human beings, this sometimes means extinction.

In modern times, the government has attempted to limit hunting and fishing seasons and the number of animals that may be taken by imposing state and federal regulations. The results have been at least partially successful. It is probable, for example, that there are more deer in North America today than there were at the time of the colonists—a fact that is not entirely good news for people whose gardens are sometimes the target of hungry herds. In effect, a rationing system (other than prices) is being used in an attempt to induce hunters and fishermen to act as though the rights to migratory animals were clearly defined, fully enforced, and readily transferable. Yet the threatened extinction of many species of whales illustrates that the problem is far from resolved.

The pattern of harvesting whales has been the subject of international discussion ever since World War II, for migratory whales are like nineteenth century bison: to own them, one must kill them. It was readily apparent to all concerned that without some form of restraint, many species of whales were in danger of extinction. The result was the founding of the International Whaling Commission (IWC) in 1948, which attempted to regulate international whaling. But the IWC was virtually doomed from the start, for its members had the right to veto any regulation they considered too restrictive, and the commission had no enforcement powers in the event a member nation chose to disregard the rules. Moreover, some whaling nations (such as Chile and Peru) refused to join the IWC, so commission quotas had little effect on them. Some IWC members have used nonmember flagships to circumvent agreed-upon quotas, while others have claimed that they were killing the whales solely for exempt "research" purposes.

The story of the decimation of a species is well told in the events surrounding blue whales, which are believed to migrate thousands of miles each year. This animal, which sometimes weighs almost a hundred tons, is difficult to kill even with the most modern equipment; nevertheless, intensive hunting gradually reduced the stock from somewhere between 300,000 and 1 million to, at present, somewhere between 600 and 3000. In the 1930–1931 winter season, almost 30,000 blue whales were taken, a number far in excess of the species' ability to replenish through reproduction. Continued intense harvesting brought the catch down to fewer than 10,000 by 1945–1946, and in the late 1950s the yearly harvest was down to around 1500 per year. By 1964–1965, whalers managed to find and kill only 20 blue whales. Despite a 1965 ban by the IWC, the hunting of blues continued by nonmembers such as Brazil, Chile, and Peru.

Humpback whales have suffered a similar fate. From an original population estimated at 300,000, there remain fewer than 5000 today. Like the blues, humpbacks are now under a hunting ban, but the lack of monitoring and enforcement capacity on the part of the IWC makes it likely that some harvesting is still taking place. IWC conservation attempts designed to protect finbacks, minke whales, and sperm whales have also been circumvented, most notably by the Russians and Japanese, who have simply announced their own unilateral quotas.

Even where government regulations attempt to protect animals, poaching has been widespread because it is a lucrative source of income. During the 1980s, the population of African elephants was cut sharply, with most of the decimation coming at the hands of poachers. In African nations where average annual income is only a few hundred dollars per person, it is little wonder that the elephant—whose tusks brought up to $6000 per pair—was a prize target of poachers. An international ban on trade in ivory has since driven the price of tusks down, offering the African elephant some respite. Yet as we saw in Chapter 4, "Sex, Booze, and Drugs," when buyer and seller are willing participants in a transaction, government bans on exchange are unlikely to be an effective long-term solution.

Nevertheless, a comparison of the experiences of various African nations suggests how a different type of government action can play a pivotal role in determining the long-term survival chances of the African elephant and other endangered species. In South Africa, where the government has allowed controlled culls (at hefty fees) and plowed the proceeds into protecting herds from poachers, the elephant population actually grew during the late 1980s, even before the ban on the ivory trade began, and continues growing today. The nation of Burundi, which exported more than 20,000 elephant tusks each year during the 1980s, provides a sharp contrast. Internationally-recognized elephant counts reveal that only one (yes, one) elephant actually lived in Burundi. Nevertheless, year after year, the government of that nation certified that all of the country's tusk exports were harvested within Burundi's borders rather than poached elsewhere. One can only wonder how that solitary, prolific pachyderm did it—and what share of the profits was going to government officials.

By taking the approach of the South African government one step further, the African nation of Zimbabwe offers some hope that the creation and enforcement of property rights in live elephants and other wildlife may ultimately protect the species from extinction. The government of Zimbabwe has established a program known as CAMPFIRE (Communal Area Programme for Indigenous Resources), which is based on the principle that the benefits from wildlife must go to those who bear the costs of having to coexist with wild animals. In effect, local inhabitants are encouraged to profit from wildlife resources. During the program's first year of existence, permits were sold to hunt 14 elephants, 82 cape buffalo, and 26 lions and leopards, generating more than $120,000 in revenues. In addition, meat from sport hunting and herd culls was distributed to the natives, who were also compensated for wildlife-caused damage to crops and livestock. There is now also a growing photographic safari industry in Zimbabwe. A report by the World Wildlife Fund estimates that the CAMPFIRE program increased household incomes by 15 to 25 percent.

The effectiveness of the CAMPFIRE program has been hampered to some extent by the resistance to change by local bureaucracies. There also has been corruption that has diverted some funds from the local inhabitants who must bear the costs of living with animals that destroy crops and people. Nevertheless, in the areas where the monies from the program are getting through, the results are striking. Poaching has all but disappeared in these regions, and land has been taken out of agricultural production to provide more wildlife habitat. The local peoples have begun to view wild animals as valuable assets, rather than solely as dangerous nuisances. As for the elephants, well, their numbers are actually growing in Zimbabwe, as local inhabitants practice conservation—not because a bureaucrat tells them they should, but because the structure of property rights makes it in their own best interest to do so.

DISCUSSION QUESTIONS

1. Has there ever been a problem with the extinction of dogs, cats, or cattle? Why not?

2. Some argue that the only way to save rare species is to set up private game reserves to which wealthy hunters can travel. How could this help save endangered species? Do you see any parallels between this proposal and the CAMPFIRE program in Zimbabwe?

3. Is government *ownership* of animals needed to protect species from extinction?

4. In the United States, most fishing streams are public property, with access available to all. In Britain, most fishing streams are privately owned, with access restricted to those who are willing to pay for the right to fish. Anglers agree that over the past 30 years, the quality of fishing in the United States has declined, while the quality of fishing in Britain has risen. Can you suggest why?

26

Smog Merchants

Pollution is undesirable, almost by definition. Most of us use the term so commonly it suggests we all know, without question, what it means. Yet there is an important sense in which "pollution is what pollution does." Consider, for example, ozone (O_3), an unstable collection of oxygen atoms. At upper levels of the atmosphere it is a naturally occurring substance that plays an essential role in protecting life from the harmful effects of ultraviolet radiation. Without the ozone layer, skin cancer would likely become a leading cause of death, and spending a day at the beach would be as healthy as snuggling up to an open barrel of radioactive waste. At lower levels of the atmosphere, however, ozone occurs as a by-product of a chemical reaction between unburned hydrocarbons (as from petroleum products), nitrogen oxides, and sunlight.[1] In this form it is a major component of smog, and breathing it can cause coughing, asthma attacks, chest pain, and possibly long-term lung-function impairment.

Consider also polychlorinated biphenyls (PCBs), molecules that exist only in man-made form. Because they are chemically quite stable, PCBs are useful in a variety of industrial applications, including insulation in large electrical transformers. Without PCBs, electricity generation would be more expensive, as would the thousands of other goods that depend on electricity for their production and distribution. Yet PCBs are also highly toxic; acute exposure (e.g., from ingestion) can result in rapid death. Chronic (long-term) exposure is suspected to cause some forms of cancer. Illegal dumping of PCBs into streams and lakes has caused mas-

---

[1] Ozone is also produced as a by-product of lightning strikes and other electrical discharges. Wherever and however it occurs, it has a distinctive metallic taste.

sive fish kills, and is generally regarded as a threat to drinking-water supplies. And since PCBs are chemically stable (i.e., they decompose very slowly), once they are released into the environment they remain a potential threat for generations to come.

As these examples suggest, the notion of pollution is highly sensitive to context. Even crude oil, so essential as a source of energy, can become pollution when it appears on the shores of Alaska's pristine beaches. Despite this fact, we shall assume in what follows that (1) we all know what pollution is when we see, smell, taste, or even read about it, and (2) holding other things constant, less of it is preferred to more.

There are numerous ways to reduce or avoid pollution. Laws can be passed banning production processes that emit pollutants into the air and water, or specifying minimum air- and water-quality levels or the maximum amount of pollution allowable. Firms would then be responsible for developing the technology and for paying the price to satisfy such standards. Or the law could specify the particular type of production technology to be used and the type of pollution-abatement equipment required in order to produce legally. Finally, subsidies could be paid to firms that reduce pollution emission, or taxes could be imposed on firms that engage in pollution emission.

No matter which methods are used to reduce pollution, costs will be incurred and problems will arise. For example, setting physical limits on the amount of pollution permitted would discourage firms from developing the technology that would reduce pollution beyond those limits. The alternative of subsidizing firms that reduce pollution levels may seem a strange use of taxpayers' dollars. The latest "solution" to the air pollution problem—selling or trading the rights to pollute—may seem even stranger. Nevertheless, this approach is now being used on a limited basis around the nation, and on a much larger scale in Los Angeles, the smog capital of the country.

Under the plan that operates in the Los Angeles area, pollution allowances have been established for 390 of the area's largest polluters. Both nitrous oxide and sulphur dioxide, the two main ingredients of Southern California's brown haze, are covered. Prior to the plan, which went into effect in 1994, the government told companies such as power plants and oil refineries what techniques they had to use to reduce pollutants. Under the new rules, companies are simply told how much they must reduce emissions each year, and they are then allowed to use whatever means they see fit to meet the standards. Over the initial ten years of the plan, firms will have their baseline emissions limits cut by 5 to 8 percent a year. By 2003, emissions of nitrous oxides from these sources should be down by 75 percent and sulphur dioxide by 60 percent.

The key element in the program is that the companies will be allowed to buy and sell "pollution rights." A firm that is successful in reducing pollutants below the levels to which it entitled receives emission reduction credits (ERCs) for doing so. The firm can sell those credits to other firms, enabling the latter to exceed their baseline emissions by the amount of credits they purchase.

Presumably, firms who can cut pollutants in the lowest-cost manner will do so, selling some of their credits to firms that find it more costly to meet the standards. Because the total level of emissions is determined ahead of time by the area's Air Quality Management District, the trading scheme will meet the requisite air quality standards. Yet because most of the emissions reductions will be made by firms that are the most efficient at doing so, the standards will be met at the lowest cost to society.

A similar market-based plan, covering only sulphur dioxide from selected sources, has been adopted by the Environmental Protection Agency (EPA) on a nationwide level. This program was kicked off by an auction of 150,000 air pollution "allowances" granted by the EPA. Each allowance permits a power utility to emit one ton of sulphur dioxide into the air. Based on their past records, utilities have been given rights to emit sulphur dioxide into the air, at a declining rate into the future. By the year 2000, utility emissions of sulphur dioxide are to be cut in half. Companies can either use their allowances to comply with the clean air regulations, or they can beat the standards and sell their unused allowances to other utilities.

The initial auction covered so-called "spot" rights for 1995, as well as "advance" rights for the year 2000. Spot prices ranged from $122 to $450 per ton, with an average price of $156. Future rights to pollute went for an average of $136 per ton, with prices ranging from $122 to $310.

Perhaps not surprisingly, the notion of selling the right to pollute has been controversial, particularly among environmental organizations. The activist group Greenpeace, for example, picketed the EPA's first auction. The group's spokesperson claimed that selling pollution allowances "is like giving a pack of cigarettes to a person dying of lung cancer." Nonetheless, other environmental groups chose to *buy* some of the allowances and thus retire them unused. One such group was the Cleveland-based National Healthy Air License Exchange, whose president said, "It is our intent . . .to have a real effect on this market and on the quality of air."

Some observers have been disappointed that the government has taken so long to approve emissions-trading schemes. There appear to be two key reasons why progress has been so slow. First, many environmentalists are vigorously opposed to the very *concept* of tradable emissions, arguing that it amounts to putting a price on what traditionally has been considered a "priceless" resource—the environment. Because most of the cost savings that stem from tradable emissions-rights accrue to the polluters and their customers, government agencies have proceeded carefully, to avoid charges that they are somehow "selling out" to polluters.

Ironically, the second reason for the delay in developing markets for tradable pollution rights has been the reluctance on the part of industry to push harder for them. Similar programs in the past have involved emissions credits that could be saved up ("banked") by a firm for later use, or bartered on a limited basis among firms. Under these earlier programs, environmental regulators have periodically simply "wiped out" emissions credits that firms thought they owned, on the ground that doing so provided a convenient means of preventing future environmental damage.

Not surprisingly, some companies believe that any credits purchased under a tradable-rights plan might be subject to the same sort of confiscation. Under such circumstances, firms have been understandably reluctant to support a program that might—or might not—prove to be of real value.[2] Indeed, even under the

---

[2] One can imagine the enthusiasm people would feel toward, say, the market for automobiles if the government announced that because cars were a source of pollution, the property rights to them might be revoked at any time, for any reason.

tradable-emissions plan adopted for Los Angeles, the regulators have explicitly stated that the emissions credits are *not* property rights, and that they can be revoked at any time. Sadly, unless obstacles such as these can be removed, achieving environmental improvement at the lowest **social cost** is likely to remain a goal rather than an accomplishment.

DISCUSSION QUESTIONS

1. Does marketing the right to pollute mean that we are allowing too much destruction of our environment?

2. Who implicitly has property rights in the air under the EPA auction system? Does your answer depend on who gets the revenue raised by the auction?

3. Some environmental groups have opposed tradable pollution-rights on the grounds that this puts a price on the environment, when in fact the environment is a "priceless" resource. Does this reasoning imply that we should be willing to give up *anything* (and therefore everything) to protect the environment? Does environmental quality have an *infinite* value? If not, how should we place a value on it?

4. Environmental regulations that prohibit emissions beyond some point implicitly allow firms and individuals to pollute up to that point at no charge. Don't such regulations amount to giving away environmental quality at no charge? Would it be better to charge a price via emissions taxes, for example, for the initial amount of pollutants? Would doing so reduce the amounts of pollution?

27

Greenhouse Economics

The sky may not be falling, but it is getting warmer—maybe. The consequences will not be catastrophic, but they will be costly—maybe. We can reverse the process, but should not spend very much to do so right now—maybe. Such is the state of the debate over the "greenhouse effect"—the apparent tendency of carbon dioxide (CO_2) and other gases to accumulate in the atmosphere, acting like a blanket that traps radiated heat, thereby increasing the earth's temperature. Before turning to the economics of the problem, let's take a brief look at the physical processes involved.

Certain gases in the atmosphere, chiefly water vapor and CO_2, trap heat radiating from the earth's surface. If they did not, the earth's average temperature would be roughly $0°$ F instead of just over $59°$ F and everything would be frozen solid. Human activity helps create some so-called greenhouse gases, including CO_2 (mainly from combustion of fossil fuels), methane (from crops and livestock), and chlorofluorocarbons (CFCs—from aerosol sprays, air conditioners, and refrigerators). We have the potential, unmatched in any other species, of profoundly altering our ecosystem.

There seems little doubt that humankind has been producing these gases at a record rate, and that they are steadily accumulating in the atmosphere. Airborne concentrations of CO_2, for example, are increasing at the rate of about 0.5 percent per year; over the past 50 years, the amount of CO_2 in the atmosphere has risen a total of about 25 percent. Laboratory analysis of glacial ice dating back at least 160,000 years indicates that global temperatures and CO_2 levels in the atmosphere do, in fact, tend to move together, suggesting that the impact of today's rising CO_2 levels may be higher global temperatures in the future. Indeed, the National Academy of Sciences (NAS) has suggested that by the middle of the twenty-first century, greenhouse gases could be double the levels they were in

1860, and that global temperatures could rise by as much as 2° to 9° F.[1] The possible consequences of such a temperature increase include the following: a rise in the average sea level, inundating coastal areas, including most of Florida; the spread of algal blooms capable of deoxygenating major bodies of water, such as the Chesapeake Bay; and the conversion of much of the midwestern wheat and corn belt into a hot, arid dust bowl.

When an individual drives a car, heats a house, or uses an aerosol hair spray, greenhouse gases are produced. In economic terms, this creates a classic **negative externality**. Most of the costs (in this case, those arising from global warming) are borne by individuals *other than* the one making the decision about how many miles to drive or how much hair spray to use. Because the driver (or sprayer) enjoys all of the benefits of the activity, but suffers only a part of the cost, that individual engages in more than the economically efficient amount of the activity. In this sense, the problem of greenhouse gases parallels the problem that occurs when someone smokes a cigarette on a crowded elevator (see Chapter 23), or litters the countryside with fast-food wrappers (see Chapter 24). If we are to get individuals to reduce production of greenhouse gases to the efficient rate, we must somehow induce them to act *as though* they bore all of the costs of their actions. The two most widely accepted means of doing this are government regulation and taxation, both of which have been proposed to deal with greenhouse gases.

The 1988 Toronto Conference on the Changing Atmosphere, attended by representatives from 48 nations, favored the regulation route. The Conference recommended a mandatory cut in CO_2 emissions by 2005 to 80 percent of their 1988 level—a move that would require a major reduction in worldwide economic output. On the taxation front, one prominent U.S. politician has proposed a tax on the carbon emitted by fuels. Under this proposal, the tax would rise to $100 per ton by the year 2000, which in turn would raise the cost of coal and oil by several hundred percent. These proposals, and others like them, clearly have the potential to reduce the buildup of greenhouse gases, but only at substantial costs. It thus makes some sense to ask: What are we likely to get for our money?

---

[1] This may not sound like much, but it does not take much to alter the world as we know it. The global average temperature at the height of the last ice age 18,000 years ago—when Canada and most of Europe were covered with ice—was 51° F, just 8° or so cooler than today.

Perhaps surprisingly, the answer to this question is not obvious. Consider, for example, the raw facts of the matter. On average over the past century, greenhouse gases have been rising and so has the average global temperature. Yet almost all of the temperature rise occurred *before* 1940, while most of the increase in greenhouse gases has occurred *after* 1940. In fact, global average temperatures fell about 0.5° F between 1940 and 1970; this cooling actually led a number of prominent scientists during the 1970s to forecast a coming ice age! Nevertheless, let us suppose for the moment that, barring a significant reduction in greenhouse gas emissions, global warming is on the way. What can we expect? According to the most comprehensive study yet of this issue, a 1991 report by the prestigious National Academy of Sciences, the answer is a "good news, bad news" story.[2]

The bad news is this: the likely rise in the sea level by 1 to 3 feet will inundate significant portions of our existing coastline; the expected decline in precipitation will necessitate more widespread use of irrigation; the higher average temperatures will compel more widespread use of air conditioning, along with the associated higher consumption of energy to power it; and the blazing heat in southern latitudes may make these areas too uncomfortable for all but the most heat-loving souls. The good news is that the technology for coping with changes such as these is well known, and the costs of coping surprisingly small—on a scale measured in terms of hundreds of billions of dollars, of course. Moreover, many of the impacts that loom large at the individual level will represent much smaller costs at a societal level. For example, although higher average temperatures could prove disastrous for farmers in southern climes, the extra warmth could be an enormous windfall farther north, where year-round farming might become feasible. Similarly, the "loss" of shoreline due to rising sea level would partly just be a migration of coastline inland—current beachfront property owners would suffer, but their inland neighbors would gain.[3]

None of these changes are free, of course, and there remain significant uncertainties about how global warming might affect

---

[2] *Policy Implications of Greenhouse Warming* (Washington: D.C., National Academy of Sciences, 1991).

[3] There would be a net loss of land area, and thus a net economic loss. Nevertheless, the net loss of land would be chiefly in the form of the (previously less valuable) inshore property that became converted into the new shoreline.

species other than *Homo sapiens.* It is estimated, for example, that temperate forests can only "migrate" at a rate of about 100 kilometers per century, not fast enough to match the speed at which warming is expected to occur. Similarly, the anticipated rise in the sea level could wipe out between 30 and 70 percent of today's coastal wetlands. Whether new wetlands would develop along our new coastline, or what might happen to species that occupy existing wetlands, are issues that have not yet been resolved.

Yet the very uncertainties that surround the possible warming of the planet suggest that radical policy prescriptions of the sort that have been proposed—such as the massive cut in worldwide CO_2 emissions advocated by the Toronto Conference—are too much, too soon. Indeed, the National Academy of Sciences recommended that we learn more before we leap too far. Some sense of the damages that can be wrought by ignoring such counsel and rushing into a politically popular response to a complex environmental issue are well illustrated by another atmospheric problem: smog.

While gasoline is a major source of the hydrocarbons in urban air, its contribution to smog is plummeting because new cars are far cleaner than their predecessors. In the 1970s, cars spewed about 9 grams of hydrocarbons per mile; emissions controls brought this down to about 1.5 grams per mile by 1995. The cost of this reduction is estimated to be approximately $1000 for each ton of hydrocarbon emissions prevented—a number that many experts believe to be well below the benefits of the cleaner air that resulted. Despite the improvements in air quality, however, smog is still a significant problem in many major cities. Additional federal regulations aimed primarily at the nine smoggiest urban areas, including New York, Chicago, and Los Angeles, went into effect in 1995. Meeting these standards meant that gasoline had to be reformulated at a cost of about 6 cents per gallon. This brought the cost of removing each additional ton of hydrocarbons to about $10,000—some 10 times the per ton cost of removing the first 95 percent from urban air. Even though many experts believe that the 1995 regulations go too far, things are scheduled to get even worse. Unless the law is modified, gasoline will have to reformulated again in the year 2000 at a cost of about 15 cents per gallon. Because so little reduction in hydrocarbons will be achievable, the cost per ton of hydrocarbons removed will exceed $200,000—roughly 200 times the per ton costs of the original reductions. Even though no one has yet come up with any estimate of benefits remotely close to these costs, we may well be stuck with enduring them, because few politicians want to be accused of being in favor of smog.

There is no doubt that atmospheric concentrations of greenhouse gases are rising, and that human actions are the cause. It is probable that, as a result, the global average temperature is, or soon will be, rising. If temperatures do rise significantly, the costs will be large but the consequences are likely to be manageable. Given the nature of the problem, private action, taken on the individual level, will not yield the optimal outcome for society. Thus the potential gains from government action, in the form of environmental regulations or taxation, are substantial. But the key word here is *potential*, for government action, no matter how well intentioned, does not automatically yield benefits that exceed the costs. As we seek solutions to the potential problems associated with greenhouse gases, we must be sure that the consequences of action are not worse than those of first examining the problem further. If we forget this message, greenhouse economics may turn into bad economics—and worse policy.

DISCUSSION QUESTIONS

1. Why will voluntary actions, undertaken at the individual level, be unlikely to bring about significant reductions in greenhouse gases such as CO_2?

2. Does the fact that the CO_2 produced in one nation results in adverse affects on other nations have any bearing on the likelihood that CO_2 emissions will be reduced to the optimal level? Would the problem be easier to solve if all of the costs and benefits were concentrated within a single country? Within a single elevator?

3. The policy approach to greenhouse gases will almost certainly involve limits on emissions, rather than taxes on emissions. Can you suggest why limits rather than taxes are likely to be used?

4. It costs about $80,000 per acre to create man-made wet-lands. How reasonable is this number as an estimate of what wetlands are worth?

Part Seven

The International Scene

INTRODUCTION

As we approach the twenty-first century, an increasing number of the public issues we face are international in character. This is as it should be, for the rapid developments in information processing, communications, and transportation over the past 20 years are gradually knitting the economies of the world closer together. Political developments, most notably the demise of the Iron Curtain and the dissolution of the Soviet Union, have contributed to this growing economic integration.

As we see in Chapter 28, "The Value of Free Trade," these developments offer both the prospects of great gain, and the risk of substantial losses. The passage of the North American Free Trade Agreement (NAFTA) and the ratification of the Uruguay round of the General Agreement on Tariffs and Trade (GATT), which created the World Trade Organization (WTO), have substantially reduced the barriers to trade between the United States and most of the rest of the world. If we take advantage of these lower trade barriers, we have the opportunity to make ourselves far better off by specializing in those activities in which we have a **comparative advantage** and then trading the fruits of our efforts with other nations. But because free trade also often redistributes wealth, in addition to creating it, there will always be some individuals who oppose free trade. Although **protectionism**—the creation of trade barriers such as tariffs and quotas—often sounds sensible, it is in fact a surefire way to reduce rather than enhance our wealth. If we ignore the value of free trade, we do so only at our own peril.

To illustrate the tremendous damages that can be wrought when protectionism gains the upper hand, Chapter 29, "The $750,000 Job," examines what happens when tariffs and quotas are imposed in an effort to "save" U.S. jobs from foreign competition. The sad facts are that: (1) in the long run, it is almost impossible to effectively protect U.S. workers from foreign competition; and (2) efforts to do so not only reduce Americans' overall living standards, but they also end up costing the jobs of other Americans. The moral of our story is that competition is just as beneficial on the international scene as it is on the domestic front.

We close in Chapter 30, "Floats, Fixes, and Crawling Pegs," with a reexamination of a theme that should be all too familiar to the readers of earlier chapters. The enormous gains that accrue from mutually beneficial exchange create forces that are generally beyond the powers of any subset of individuals—or even governments—to master. What is true for drugs, abortion, water, and apartments is just as true for the currencies in which international exchange is conducted. Politicians may pass legislation, and bureaucrats may do their best to enforce it, but the laws of demand and supply ultimately rule the economy—even when that economy encompasses the entire world.

28

The Value of Free Trade

The decade of the 1990s has been a time of great change on the international trade front. The North American Free Trade Agreement (NAFTA), for example, has substantially reduced the barriers to trade among citizens of Canada, the United States, and Mexico. On a global scale, the Uruguay round of the General Agreement on Tariffs and Trade (GATT) was ratified by 117 nations including the United States. Under the terms of this agreement, GATT is replaced by the World Trade Organization (WTO), and tariffs are being cut worldwide by 40 percent. Agricultural subsidies will be reduced, patent protections extended worldwide, and the WTO will establish a set of arbitration boards to settle international disputes over trade issues.

Many economists believe that both NAFTA and the agreements reached during the Uruguay round were victories not only for free trade but also for the citizens of the participating nations. Nevertheless, many noneconomists, particularly politicians, opposed these agreements, so it is important we understand what is beneficial about NAFTA, the Uruguay round, and free trade in general.

Opposition to free trade is nothing new on the American political landscape. In this century, one of the most famous examples of such opposition was the Smoot–Hawley Tariff of 1930. This major federal government statute was a classic example of **protectionism**—an effort to protect a subset of American producers at the expense of consumers and other producers. It included **tariff** schedules for over 20,000 products, raising tariffs on affected imports by an average of 52 percent.

The Smoot–Hawley Tariff encouraged "beggar-thy-neighbor" policies by the rest of the world. Such policies represent an attempt to improve (a portion of) one's domestic economy at the expense of foreign countries' economies. An example is the imposition of a tariff to discourage imports, in the hopes that a domestic import-competing industry will benefit. The beggar-thy-neighbor policy at the heart of the Smoot–Hawley Tariff Act of 1930 was soon adopted by the United Kingdom, France, the Netherlands, and Switzerland. The result was a massive reduction in international trade. According to many economists, this caused a worsening of the ongoing worldwide depression of the period.

Opponents of free trade seem to accept the notion that beggar-thy-neighbor policy would somehow benefit the United States. What these opponents forget, however, is one of the most fundamental propositions in international trade: *In the long run, imports are paid for by exports*. This proposition simply states that when one country buys goods and services from the rest of the world (imports), the rest of the world eventually wants goods from that country (exports) in exchange. Given this fundamental proposition, a corollary becomes obvious: *Any restriction on imports leads to a reduction in exports*. Thus, any business for import-competing industries gained as a result of tariff means at least as much business *lost* for exporting industries.

Given that this is true, it immediately raises the question: How does legislation like the Smoot–Hawley Tariff ever get passed? As Mark Twain stated many years ago, the reason the free traders win the arguments and the protectionists win the votes is because foreign competition often clearly affects a narrow and specific import-competing industry such as textiles, shoes, or automobiles. Because of the concentrated benefits that accrue when Congress votes in favor of trade restrictions, sufficient monies can be raised in those industries to convince Congress to impose the restrictions.

The eventual reduction in exports that must follow is normally spread in small doses throughout all export industries. Thus, no specific group of workers, managers, or shareholders in export industries will feel that it should contribute money to convince Congress to *reduce* international trade restrictions. Additionally, consumers of imports and import-competing goods lose due to trade restrictions, but they too are a large, diffuse group of individuals, none of whom will be affected a great deal because of any single import restriction. It is the simultaneous existence of concentrated benefits and diffuse costs that led to Mark Twain's conclusion that the protectionists would normally win the votes.

Another key point in the debate over free trade involves simple balance of payments accounting. In brief, the **current account** part of the balance of payments is a summary of a country's dealings with the rest of the world with respect to goods and services (and gifts). A country's **capital account** involves its dealings with the rest of the world with respect to investments and lending.

In a world of floating exchange rates, there is only one way for one country to receive positive net investment from the rest of the world: *It has to be in deficit on its current account.* Indeed, if a country has floating exchange rates, its current account deficit will be exactly offset by a surplus in its capital account. After all, for foreigners to invest in the United States, they need dollars. Those extra dollars can only be generated by Americans buying more goods and services from other countries than foreigners buy from Americans. The difference—the current account deficit—represents a supply of dollars to the rest of the world, which the rest of the world can use to invest in America.

Thus, a discussion of whether or not America will run a balance of trade deficit or surplus with any nation because of free trade agreements is largely irrelevant. Indeed, concerns about balance of payments deficits or surpluses with any country, at any time, are always irrelevant. Any current account deficit is always matched by a surplus in the capital account. This is the way we have net investment by foreigners; actually, it is the only way we can continue to have positive net investment from the rest of the world. There is no necessarily beneficial side to a favorable balance of trade. After all, a deficit on current account—an "unfavorable" balance of trade—means that there will be positive net foreign investment; this adds to our capital stock and may add to our productivity and hence to a higher standard of living in the future.

Many of the arguments pushed by the opponents of free trade are implicitly based on the notion that international trade is a **zero-sum game**—that is, a process in which what one party gains, the other must lose. But if that were true, then all exchange would be a zero-sum game, for international trade is simply an extension of voluntary individual exchange. In fact, voluntary individual exchange only occurs because, beforehand, both parties believe that they will be better off after the trade.

Voluntary trade creates new wealth. In voluntary trade, both parties in an exchange gain. They give up something of lesser value in return for something of greater value. In this sense, exchanges are always unequal. But it is this unequal nature of exchange that is the source of the increased productivity that occurs whenever trade takes place. For example, imagine that you are willing to exchange a bushel of apples from your orchard for a bushel of oranges from our grove. This means that you value our bushel of oranges more than your bushel of apples. Through trade you use your apples to obtain something that you wanted but did not have before—a bushel of or-anges. Therefore, you are made better off. If you didn't think you would become better off, you never would have entered into the exchange.

Free trade encourages individuals to employ their talents and abilities in the most productive manner possible, and to exchange the fruits of their efforts. The **gains from trade** lie in one of the most fun-damental ideas in economics—a nation gains from doing what it can do best *relative* to other nations, that is, by specializing in those en-deavors in which it has a **comparative advantage**. Trade encourages individuals and nations to discover ways to specialize so that they can become more productive and enjoy higher incomes. Increased pro-ductivity and the subsequent increase in the rate of economic growth are exactly what the signatories of the Uruguay round and NAFTA seek by reducing trade barriers.

Because trades typically do result in both parties being better off—that is, trade is a **positive-sum game**—individuals continue to voluntarily engage in exchange. The same is true with respect to trade between and among the 50 states in the union. Why would it no longer be true simply because "foreigners" are in-volved? International trade is not a zero-sum game.

Despite the gains that result from free trade, a statistical study of the cost of protectionism might give the impression that taxes on imported goods simply raise their price to domestic consumers. But there is another cost that may be hidden. It is what might be called the **Type II error** associated with protec-tionism. In statistics, a **Type I error** is the cost of *commission*—for example, as discussed in Chapter 1, a drug put on the market-place may cause adverse side effects. In contrast, a Type II error is the cost of *omission*—for example, if a drug is not put on the marketplace, some individuals may suffer longer, and some may die.

The Type II error associated with protectionism, like the Type II error associated with *not* introducing beneficial drugs, is equally insidious, because we have a difficult time statistically tracing "what might have been." What happens when trade is re-stricted is that the protectionist country is deprived of a poten-tially large range of new goods and production processes. Such new foreign products could and can spur local support businesses, which in turn cause other businesses to be created. For example, if a developing country restricts entry of computer products, it will slow the development of its own software industry. Even in the United States, had we more severely restricted the imports of Japanese and German automobiles over the last 20 years, the American automobile industry would not have been forced to improve domestically produced cars. Had the People's Republic of China and the former Soviet Union not allowed McDonald's to build restaurants, those countries would have taken longer to see how products can be served in an efficient, clean, and friendly environment.

How important is the Type II error associated with protectionism? Few economists have statistically studied this issue. But some evidence comes from what has actually happened because we implemented NAFTA, and thus avoided a Type II error. The portion of this treaty that applies to U.S. trade with Canada dates back to 1988. Since that time, U.S.–Canadian trade has soared more than 40%. Overall, Canada is our leading trading partner, with exports and imports each in the range of $100 billion per year.

In light of numbers such as these, we can expect the parties to the Uruguay round and NAFTA to grow faster than they would have had these treaties not been adopted. The United States certainly will not experience increases in economic growth as great as will be enjoyed by some of the smaller, historically protectionist signatories of the Uruguay round. Nevertheless, both economic theory and empirical evidence indicate that, on balance, Americans will be better off after—and because of—the move to freer trade.

DISCUSSION QUESTIONS

1. What effect would a U.S. import tariff have on the value of the U.S. dollar on world currency markets?

2. What effect would a rise in the value of the dollar have on the ability of American firms to export their goods?

3. The U.S. government currently forbids the export of oil from Alaska to foreign countries. What effect does this have on American *imports*?

4. Is it ever possible for the imposition of an import tariff by the United States to make citizens of the United States better off?

29

The $750,000 Job

In even-numbered years, particularly years evenly divisible by four, politicians of all persuasions are apt to give long-winded speeches about the need to protect U.S. jobs from the evils of foreign competition. To accomplish this goal, we are encouraged to "Buy American." If further encouragement is needed, we are told that if we do not voluntarily reduce the amount of imported goods we purchase, the government will impose (or make more onerous) either **tariffs** (taxes) on imported goods or **quotas** (quantity restrictions) that physically limit imports. The objective of this exercise is to "save" U.S. jobs.

Unlike African elephants or blue whales, U.S. jobs are in no danger of becoming extinct. There are an infinite number of potential jobs in the American economy, and there always will be. Some of these jobs are not very pleasant, and many others do not pay very well, but there will always be employment of some sort as long as there is scarcity. Thus, when an autoworker making $45,000 per year says that imports of Japanese cars should be reduced to save his job, what he really means is this: He wants to be protected from competition so that he can continue his present employment at the same or higher salary, rather than move to a different employment that has less desirable working conditions or pays a lower salary. There is nothing wrong with the autoworker's goal (better working conditions and higher pay), but it has nothing to do with "saving" jobs. (Despite this, we may even use the term in the discussion that follows, because it is such convenient shorthand.)

In any discussion of the consequences of restrictions on international trade, it is essential to remember two facts. First, *we pay for imports with exports.* It is true that, in the short run, we can sell off assets or borrow from abroad if we happen to import more

188

goods and services than we export. But we have only a finite amount of assets to sell, and foreigners do not want to wait forever before we pay our bills. Ultimately, our accounts can be settled only if we *provide* (export) goods and services to the trading partners from whom we *purchase* (import) goods and services. Trade, after all, involves *quid pro quo* (literally, "something for something"). The second point to remember is that *voluntary trade is mutually beneficial to the trading partners.* If we restrict international trade, we reduce those benefits, both for our trading partners and for ourselves. One way these reduced benefits are manifested is in the form of curtailed employment opportunities for workers. In a nutshell, even though tariffs and quotas enhance job opportunities in import-competing industries, they also cost us jobs in export industries; the net effect seems to be reduced employment overall.

What is true for the United States is true for other countries as well: They will only buy our goods if they can market theirs, since they too have to export goods to pay for their imports. Thus, any U.S. restrictions on imports to this country—via tariffs, quotas, or other means—ultimately causes a reduction in our exports, because other countries will be unable to pay for our goods. This implies that import restrictions inevitably must decrease the size of our export sector. So imposing trade restrictions to save jobs in import-competing industries has the effect of costing jobs in export industries.

Just as important, import restrictions impose costs on U.S. consumers as a whole. By reducing competition from abroad, quotas, tariffs, and other trade restraints push up the prices of foreign goods and enable U.S. producers to hike their own prices. Perhaps the best documented example of this is found in the automobile industry, where "voluntary" restrictions on Japanese imports have been in place for more than a decade.

Due in part to the enhanced quality of imported cars, sales of domestically produced automobiles fell from 9 million units in 1978 to an average of 6 million units per year between 1980 and 1982. Profits of U.S. automobile manufacturers plummeted as well, turning into substantial losses for some of them. United States automobile manufacturers and autoworkers' unions demanded protection from import competition. They were joined in their cries by politicians from automobile-producing states. The result was a "voluntary" agreement entered into by Japanese car companies (the most important competitors of U.S. firms), which restricted U.S. sales of Japanese cars to 1.68 million units per year. This agreement—which amounted to a quota, even though it never officially bore that name—began in April 1981 and continued into the 1990s in various forms.

Robert W. Crandall, an economist with the Brookings Institute, has estimated how much this voluntary trade restriction has cost U.S. consumers in terms of higher car prices. According to his estimates, the reduced supply of Japanese cars pushed their prices up by $1,500 apiece, measured in 1996 dollars. The higher price of Japanese imports in turn enabled domestic producers to hike their prices an average of $600 per car. The total tab in the first full year of the program was $6.5 billion—and in recent years it likely has been even greater. Crandall also estimated the number of jobs in automobile-related industries that were saved by the voluntary import restrictions; the total was about 26,000. Dividing $6.5 billion by 26,000 jobs yields a cost to consumers of better than $250,000 *per year* for every job saved in the automobile industry. United States consumers could have saved nearly $2 billion on their car purchases each year if, instead of implicitly agreeing to import restrictions, they had simply given $75,000 to every autoworker whose job was preserved by the voluntary import restraints.

The same types of calculations have been made for other industries. Tariffs in the apparel industry were increased between 1977 and 1981, saving the jobs of about 116,000 U.S. apparel workers at a cost of $45,000 per job each year. At about the same time, the producers of citizens band (CB) radios also managed to get tariffs raised. Approximately 600 workers in the industry kept their jobs as a result, but at an annual cost to consumers of over $85,000 per job. The cost of protectionism has been even higher in other industries. Jobs preserved in the glassware industry due to trade restrictions cost $200,000 apiece each year. In the maritime industry, the yearly cost of trade protection is $270,000 per job. In the steel industry, the cost of preserving a job has been estimated at an astounding $750,000 *per year*. If free trade were permitted, each worker losing a job could be given a cash payment of half that amount each year, and the consumer would still save a lot of money.

Even so, this is not the full story. None of these studies estimating the cost to consumers of saving jobs in import-competing industries has attempted to estimate the ultimate impact of import restrictions on the flow of exports, the number of jobs in the export sector, and thus the total number of jobs gained or lost.

When imports to the United States are restricted, our trading partners can afford to buy less of what we produce. The resultant decline in export sales means fewer jobs in exporting industries. And the total reduction in trade leads to fewer jobs for workers such as stevedores (who unload ships) and truck drivers (who carry goods to and from ports). On both counts—the overall cut in trade and the accompanying decline in exports—protectionism leads to job losses that might not be obvious immediately.

In 1983, Congress tried to pass a "domestic content" bill for automobiles. In effect, the legislation would have required that cars sold in the United States have a minimum percentage of their components manufactured and assembled in this country. Proponents of the legislation argued that it would have protected 300,000 jobs in the U.S. automobile manufacturing and auto parts supply industries. Yet the legislation's supporters failed to recognize the negative impact of the bill on trade in general, and its ultimate impact on U.S. export industries. A U.S. Department of Labor study did recognize these impacts, estimating that the domestic content legislation would actually cost more jobs in trade-related and export industries than it protected in import-competing businesses. Congress ultimately decided not to impose a domestic content requirement for cars sold in the United States.

In principle, trade restrictions are imposed to provide economic help to specific industries and to increase employment in those industries. Ironically, the long-term effects may be just the opposite. Researchers at the General Agreement on Tariffs and Trade (GATT) in Switzerland have examined employment in three industries that have been heavily protected throughout the world—textiles, clothing, and iron and steel. Despite stringent trade protection for these industries, employment actually declined during the period of protection, in some cases dramatically. In textiles employment fell 22 percent in the United States and 46 percent in the European Common Market. The clothing industry had employment losses ranging from 18 percent in the United States to 56 percent in Sweden. Declines in employment in the

iron and steel industry ranged anywhere from 10 percent in
Canada to 54 percent in the United States. In short, GATT researchers found that restrictions on free trade were no guarantee
against job losses—even in the industries supposedly being
protected.

The evidence seems clear: the cost of protecting jobs in the
short run is enormous. And in the long run, it appears that jobs
cannot be protected, especially if one considers all aspects of protectionism. Free trade is a tough platform on which to run for office. But it looks as if it is the one that will yield the most general
benefits if implemented; of course, this does not mean that politicians will embrace it. And so we ending up "saving" jobs at a cost
of $750,000 each.

DISCUSSION QUESTIONS

1. Who gains and who loses from import restrictions?

2. What motivates politicians to impose tariffs, quotas, and other
    trade restrictions?

3. If it would be cheaper to give each steelworker $375,000 per
    year in cash than impose restrictions on imports of steel, why do
    we have the import restrictions rather than the cash payments?

4. Most U.S. imports and exports travel through our seaports at
    some point. How do you predict that members of Congress
    from coastal states would vote on proposals restrict interna-
    tional trade? What other information would you want to know
    in making such a prediction?

30

Floats, Fixes, and Crawling Pegs

Ask just about any economist and the response will be the same: government attempts to control market prices are costly and almost certainly destined for failure. Yet some economists, and many bureaucrats in the business of international finance, would argue that **exchange rates**—the prices at which the world currencies trade—should be controlled by governments. As Robert Mundell, a Columbia University economist puts it, "The flexible exchange rate system has not worked. . . . We need a new [system] to restore order." One French finance minister says it almost as succinctly: "The system has been a failure, proving devoid of discipline or constraints, much too tolerant of poorly managed economies and ultimately harmful for the world economy." Wait a minute: if, as most observers would agree, government price controls are unlikely to succeed, why do so many want to control the price of nations' currencies? The answer goes back a long way.

Sometime in history—at least five thousand years ago, and possibly as much as ten thousand years in the past—people began using precious metals as the foundation for their monetary systems. Gold was the most popular metal, but silver and even copper were also used. The reason was simple: governments seemed irresistibly tempted to debase and thereby cheapen the currencies they issued by pumping out more and more of it. This pushed up the inflation rate and drove down the value of the currency—sometimes far enough to make it worthless. But when precious metals were used as money, the government couldn't simply turn on the printing presses if it wanted more money. Instead, it had to "earn it the old-fashioned way"—by direct taxation.

Using precious metals as currency, however, instead of enjoying them in the form of jewelry or other consumables, is expensive. So people decided to go to a system in which governments were allowed to issue paper currency, but were required to "peg" or "fix" the value of the paper currency to a precious metal such as gold. Governments were prevented from issuing excessive amounts of paper currency by having to hold reserves of gold or silver in their treasuries, and to redeem the currency "on demand" with specified amounts of the precious metals. If a government tried to issue too much paper money, people would simply exchange it for gold or silver, thereby ridding the country of the excess currency. If not enough currency were issued, people could bring in gold or silver and exchange it for new currency. In this way, currency supplies were kept at levels that ensured generally stable price levels.

(There were two exceptions to the rule of stable price levels. First, during wartime, people often allowed their government to suspend the free exchange of paper currency for gold or silver, enabling the government to issue more currency to finance the fighting. Not surprisingly, inflation has been a common feature of wartime. Second, there were periodic discoveries of new supplies of gold or silver—most notably in the sixteenth and nineteenth centuries—which pushed up government reserves of the metals. These added reserves allowed governments to issue more money, which in turn eventually created inflation.)

Over time, some countries gained a reputation for being particularly reliable in keeping the value of their currencies stable. For many years, Great Britain was the leader in this role; during the twentieth century, America became a major player. Other countries, noting the stability of the British pound sterling and the U.S. dollar, decided to "peg" the value of their currencies to them, rather than to the value of specific precious metals. Perhaps the most famous example of this was the Bretton Woods Agreement, entered into shortly after World War II: signatories agreed to go to a system of **fixed exchange rates**. In effect, most of the free world nations said they would tie (i.e., fix) the value of their currencies to the U.S. dollar.

For twenty years, the system seemed to work well. But in the late 1960s and early 1970s, the United States began "printing money" to help finance the Vietnam War. This fueled inflation in America and put downward pressure on the value of the dollar relative to other currencies. Other countries were forced to increase supplies of their own currencies to keep the value of the dollar from dropping below the bounds of the Bretton Woods Agreement. This pushed up inflation around the world, and ultimately led to an abandonment of the system of fixed exchange rates; Western Europe and Japan were not willing to keep their currencies tied to the dollar if it meant tolerating high inflation.

When the Bretton Woods Agreement was abandoned in the early 1970s, free world countries opted for a system of **flexible, or floating, exchange rates**, in which the relative prices of the world's currencies were free to move in response to supply and demand. If a country came up with an appealing export product—as Japan did with automobiles—the value of that country's currency would tend to rise. Simply put, if American car dealers wanted to buy Japanese autos, they first had to buy Japanese yen to pay for them. This increase in the demand for yen drove up its price (other factors held constant). Conversely, if a country had a poor agricultural harvest and thus imported more food from other nations, this drove down the value of its currency: paying for the added imports required the country to sell more of its currency.

The move to floating exchange rates has most definitely proved them to be flexible. On a baseline scale of 100 (relative to other world currencies), the U.S. dollar fell from 120 in 1971 to 95 in the late 1970s, rose to 150 in 1985, and plunged to near 100 by the end of the 1980s and then rose again in the early 1990s. Over the same period, the Japanese yen went from under 80 to nearly 110, plummeted to 85, and then soared to over 200. Even in Western Europe, where the economies are as closely tied as any in the world, currency gyrations have been evident. During the 1980s, for example, the French franc fell in value by nearly one-third relative to the German mark.

Although many economists applauded the move to flexible exchange rates, some people found it objectionable—on two markedly different grounds. First, most people dislike competition, especially when it comes from citizens of other nations. Floating exchange rates have enhanced the feeling of competitiveness among firms in different countries, thus producing resentment. When the value of the dollar rises—making American goods expensive and foreign goods cheap—U.S. importers are happy, but American exporters complain bitterly that the value of the dollar should be "stabilized." When the value of the dollar falls—making American goods attractive for purchase abroad and foreign goods expensive in this country—exporters stop complaining, but U.S. importers cry that the value of the dollar should be "stabilized." The same sort of responses are heard in other nations when the values of their currencies fluctuate: many people object when the price of their currency rises; others complain when it falls; none, it seems, are happy all the time. The result has been intense pressure on governments around the world to prevent floating exchange rates from being *quite* so flexible. As one senior official put it: "Everybody loves competition—but only when they are the beneficiaries and the other guy is the one who actually has to compete."

The second—and perhaps less cynical—reason for objecting to floating exchange rates is that flexible rates fail to sufficiently discipline the world's governments. When a country is on a fixed exchange rate system it must keep the value of its currency closely aligned with that of a precious metal or the currency of another country. Thus, it cannot casually pursue whatever set of monetary or fiscal policies are currently most politically convenient. If it inflates its money supply too fast, the value of its currency will start to fall—meaning that it will have cut back on its money supply to bring its currency value in line with the agreed-upon exchange rate. If it borrows too much, interest rates will rise, making its currency attractive to foreign citizens. As foreigners buy the currency, its value rises and the country again has to moderate its policies to keep the foreign exchange value of its currency stable.

Under flexible exchange rates, this direct discipline is missing. Countries can inflate or deflate at will, helping to cause the fluctuations in exchange rates witnessed during the past 20 years. In an effort to restore at least some semblance of control, several European nations adopted a so-called "crawling peg" system, in which exchange rates among their currencies were supposed to fluctuate within a band of plus or minus 2.25 percent. But the crawling peg has been less than a spectacular success. Despite heavy central bank intervention—by buying or selling huge amounts of various currencies—there have been at least a dozen revaluations of European Monetary System (EMS) member currencies.

The problem that these European nations have faced boils down to one central issue: how to prevent market forces from doing what comes naturally. This, indeed, is the principal problem facing all governments in their efforts to control exchange rates. Wars, oil embargoes, droughts, monetary policies, and even technological innovations, all affect the supply of and demand for currencies around the world. The changes occur day-by-day, hour-by-hour, minute-by-minute. The action is heavy, and swift enough to keep thousands of foreign exchange dealers (and their millions of clients) busy in every corner of the world. The chances are minuscule that a few central bankers or finance ministers could possibly keep up with the myriad bits of information that drive the supply of and demand for the world's currencies. And even if they did, the best they could hope for would be an outcome that would have been produced by the market system anyway. There are simply too many billions of dollars (and marks, yen, francs, and pounds sterling) floating around in foreign exchange markets for any single government (or even groups of governments) to hope to control their prices. Unless and until all of the world's governments agree to adopt a single currency for common use (a most unlikely event), fixed exchange rates and crawling pegs will surface occasionally, but it appears that floating rates are here to stay.

DISCUSSION QUESTIONS

1. During the late 1980s and early 1990s American automobile manufacturers greatly increased the quality of the cars they produced, relative to the quality of the cars produced in other nations. What effect would this have on the value of the American dollar on world currency markets?

2. During the 1980s some Japanese automakers opened plants in the United States so that they could produce (and sell) "Japanese" cars in the United States. What effect would this have had on the value of the U.S. dollar?

3. Japanese carmakers voluntarily limit the number of cars they import into the U.S. If this voluntary import quota were eliminated, what do you think would happen to the value of the Japanese yen?

4. How would a difference in the inflation rates in Canada and the United States affect the relative values of the two nations' currencies?

GLOSSARY

Bond: An interest-bearing certificate issued by a government or a corporation. This type of security represents debt.

Capital account: A record of the loans and investments made by a nation during a specified accounting period. If the value of the loans and investments made abroad is less than the value made domestically by foreign individuals, businesses, and governments, the account is said to be in surplus; if this inequality is reversed, the account is in deficit. See also *current account.*

Cartel: A group of independent industrial corporations, often on an international scale, that agree to restrict trade, to their mutual benefit.

Common stock: A security that indicates real ownership in a corporation. A common stock is not a legal obligation for the firm and does not have a date of maturity. It has the last claim on dividends each year, and on assets in the event of the firm's liquidation.

Comparative advantage: The ability to produce goods at a lower cost.

Competition: Rivalry among buyers and sellers of outputs, or among buyers and sellers of inputs.

Current account: A record of the exports and imports of goods, services, and unilateral transfers (gifts) for a nation during a specified accounting period. If the value of the exports exceeds the value of the imports, the account is said to be in surplus; if imports exceed exports, the account is in deficit. See also capital account.

Demand curve: A graphic representation of the demand schedule; a negatively sloped line showing the inverse relationship between the price and the quantity demanded.

Demand schedule: A set of number pairs showing various possible prices and the quantities demanded at each price. This schedule shows the rate of planned purchases per time period at different prices of the good.

Disposable, or contingent, worker: An individual without permanent employment status, who generally has reduced job security and works for lower pay and without the full range of fringe benefits.

Economic good: Any good or service that is scarce.

Elastic demand: A characteristic of a demand curve in which a given percentage change in price will result in a larger inverse percentage change in quantity demanded. Total revenues and price are inversely related in the elastic portion of the demand curve.

Elasticity of demand: The responsiveness of the quantity of a commodity demanded to a change in its price per unit. See also *Price elasticity of demand.*

Elasticity of supply: The responsiveness of the quantity of a commodity supplied to a change in its price per unit. See also *Price elasticity of supply.*

Equilibrium price: The price that clears the market when there is no excess quantity demanded or supplied; the price at which the demand curve intersects the supply curve. Also called *Market-clearing price.*

Exchange rates: The prices at which currencies of different nations trade, usually expressed in terms of the number of units of one currency that it takes to purchase another currency.

Expansion: A business fluctuation in which overall business activity is rising at a more rapid rate than in a previous time period, or at a more rapid rate than the overall historical trend in a particular country.

Externalities: A situation in which a benefit or a cost associated with an economic activity spills over to a third party. Pollution is a negative spillover, or externality.

Fixed exchange rates: The prices at which currencies of different nations trade, decided upon and adhered to by the governments of the nations involved. Maintenance of fixed exchange rates generally requires the governments to alter the supplies of their currencies in a manner that is consistent with the agreed-upon fixed rate.

Flexible, or floating, exchange rates: The prices at which currencies of different nations trade. The prices are allowed to fluctuate in accord with the forces of demand and supply, without interference by governments.

Free good: Any good or service available in larger quantities than desired at a zero price.

Gains from trade: The extent to which individuals, firms, or nations benefit by engaging in exchange.

Gross domestic product (GDP): The dollar value of all of a nation's new, domestically-produced final goods and services within a specified accounting period, usually a year.

Income distribution: The way income is distributed among the population. For example, a perfectly equal distribution of income would result in the lowest 20 percent of income earners receiving 20 percent of national income and the top 20 percent also receiving 20 percent of national income. The middle 60 percent of income earners would receive 60 percent of national income.

Income mobility: The tendency of individuals' incomes to change relative to the incomes of other people over time, most commonly caused by the fact that individuals' incomes tend to grow more rapidly than average up to age 40 or 45, grow more slowly than average up to age 55, and then begin to decline.

Inelastic demand: A characteristic of a demand curve in which a given change in price will result in a less-than-proportionate inverse change in the quantity demanded. Total revenue and price are directly related in the inelastic region of the demand curve.

Inflation: A sustained rise in the weighted average of all prices over time.

In-kind transfers: Items of value other than money that are given to individuals by the government, such as medical care, housing, and food.

Inside information: Any information that is available only to a few people, such as officers of a corporation.

Labor force participation rate: The percentage of the population (usually of a specified age, such as 16 or older) that is either working or is unemployed but actively seeking and available for work.

Law of demand: A law stating that quantity demanded and price are inversely related—more is bought at a lower price, less at a higher price (other things being equal).

Law of supply: A law that states that a direct relationship exists between price and quantity supplied (other things being equal).

Marginal analysis: The analysis of what happens when small changes take place relative to the status quo.

Marginal benefits: The additional (marginal) benefits associated with one more unit of a good or action; the change in total benefits due to the addition of one more unit of production.

Marginal costs: The change in total costs due to a change in one unit of production.

Marginal product: The additional output obtained by using one more unit of an input.

Marginal revenue: The additional revenue obtained from selling one more unit of output.

Marginal revenue product: The additional revenue obtained as a result of using one more unit of an input; it equals the *marginal revenue* obtained from selling another unit of output, multiplied by the *marginal product* of the input.

Market-clearing price: See **Equilibrium price.**

Market supply: Total quantities of a good offered for sale by suppliers at various prices.

Median age: The age that exactly separates the younger half of the population from the older half.

Minimum wage: The lowest hourly wage firms may legally pay their workers.

Models, or theories: Simplified representations of the real world used to make predictions or to better understand the real world.

Monopolist, or **Monopoly:** Literally, a single supplier. More generally, it is a firm that faces a downward-sloping demand curve for its output, and therefore can choose the price at which it will sell the good; an example of a *price searcher.*

Monopsonist, or **Monopsony:** Literally, a single buyer. More generally, it is a firm that faces a upward-sloping supply curve for its input, and therefore can choose the price at which it will buy the good; an example of a *price searcher.*

Negative externality: A cost, associated with an economic activity, which is paid by third parties. Pollution is a negative externality because, for example, someone other than the driver of an automobile bears part of the cost of the car's exhaust emissions.

Opportunity cost: The highest-valued alternative that must be sacrificed to attain something or to satisfy a want.

Per capita income: Total income divided by population.

Perfectly elastic: An infinite value for the ratio of the percentage change in quantity over the percentage change in price, measured along a demand or supply curve; visually, a perfectly elastic curve appears horizontal.

Portfolio: An assortment of stocks or bonds owned by an individual. Generally, the riskiness of a portfolio is lower than the riskiness of any of the individual stocks or bonds in the portfolio.

Positive-sum game: A process or setting in which more than one participant gains. Voluntary exchange is said to be a positive-sum game because both parties are simultaneously made better-off.

Preferred stock: A security that indicates financing obtained from investors by a corporation. Preferred stock is not a legal obligation for the firm and does not have a date of maturity, but pays a fixed dividend each year. It has preferred position over common stock, both for dividends and for assets in the event of the firm's liquidation.

Price elasticity of demand: The percentage change in quantity demanded divided by the percentage change in price. See also *Elasticity of demand*.

Price elasticity of supply: The percentage change in quantity supplied divided by the percentage change in price. See also *Elasticity of supply*.

Price searcher: Literally, a firm that must search for the profit-maximizing price, because it faces a downward-sloping demand curve (if it is a seller) or an upward-sloping supply curve (if it is a buyer); often used as a synonym for *monopoly* or *monopsony*.

Price taker: Any economic agent that takes the market price as given; often used as a synonym for a firm operating in a market characterized by *pure competition*.

Profit: The income generated by selling something for a higher price than was paid for it. In production, the income generated is the difference between total revenues received from consumers who purchase the goods and the total cost of producing those goods.

Property rights: The set of rules specifying how a good may be used and exchanged.

Protectionism: A set of rules designed to protect certain individuals or firms from competition, usually competition from imported goods.

Public information: Any kind of information that is widely available to the public.

Pure competition: A market structure in which participants individually have no influence over market prices; all act as *price takers*.

Quotas: Limits on the amount of a good or activity; often used in international trade to limit the amount of some foreign good that legally may be imported into a country.

Random walk: The situation in which future behavior cannot be predicted from past behavior. Stock prices follow a random walk.

Rate of return: The net benefit, in percentage terms, of engaging in an activity. For example, if the investment of $1 yields a gross return of $1.20, the net benefit is $0.20 and the rate of return is equal to ($0.20/$1.00) = 20 percent.

Recession: A period of time during which the rate of growth of business activity is consistently less than its long-term trend is negative.

Rent control: A system in which the government tells building owners how much they can charge for rent.

Resource: An input used in the production of desired goods and services.

Scarce good: Any good that commands a positive price.

Scarcity: A state of nature in which resources are limited even though wants are unlimited. Scarcity means that nature does not freely provide as much of everything as people want.

Share of stock: Legal claim to a share of the future profits of a corporation.

Shareholder: The owner of *shares of stock*.

Shortage: A situation in which an excess quantity is demanded or an insufficient quantity is supplied; the difference between the quantity demanded and the quantity supplied at a specific price below the market-clearing price.

Social cost: The full cost that society bears when a resource-using action occurs. For example, the social cost of driving a car is equal to all private costs plus any additional cost that society bears (e.g., air pollution and traffic congestion).

Stock: The quantity of something at a point in time. An inventory of goods is a stock. A bank account at a point in time is a stock. Stocks are defined independent of time, although they are assessed at a point in time. See also *share of stock*.

Stockbroker: An individual who acts as a middleman in the market for corporate stocks and bonds, enabling potential buyers and sellers of those stocks and bonds to engage in exchange.

Supply curve: The graphic representation of the supply schedule, which slopes upward (has a positive slope).

Supply schedule: A set of prices and the quantity supplied at each price; a schedule showing the rate of planned production at each relative price for a specified time period.

Surplus: An excess quantity supplied or an insufficient quantity demanded; the difference between the quantity supplied and the quantity demanded at a price above the market-clearing price.

Tariffs: Taxes levied on imports.

Trade barriers: Any rules having the effect of reducing the amount of international exchange. *Tariffs* and *quotas* are trade barriers.

Trade-off: A term relating to opportunity cost. In order to get a desired economic good, it is necessary to trade off some other desired economic good in a situation of scarcity. A trade-off involves making a sacrifice in order to obtain something.

Type I error: An error of commission, such as might arise when an unsafe drug is errantly permitted to be sold.

Type II error: An error of omission, such as might arise if a beneficial drugs is errantly prevented from reaching the market.

Vouchers: Government subsidies that can be used only to purchase specified goods, such as education or housing.

Zero-sum game: A process or setting in which what one participant gains, another must lose; thus, both cannot simultaneously gain or lose.

Index